CONTENTS

Newsletters 3

   Welcome Letter (English) 5

   Boletín (Spanish) 6

   Theme 1: Silly Stories (English) 7

   Theme 1: Cuentos cómicos (Spanish) 8

   Theme 2: Nature Walk (English) 9

   Theme 2: Vamos afuera (Spanish) 10

   Theme 3: Around Town:

      Neighborhood and Community (English) 11

   Theme 3: Vivimos aquí (Spanish) 12

   Theme 4: Amazing Animals (English) 13

   Theme 4: Animales asombrosos (Spanish) 14

   Theme 5: Family Time (English) 15

   Theme 5: En familia (Spanish) 16

   Theme 6: Talent Show (English) 17

   Theme 6: ¡Aplausos! (Spanish) 18

Selection Summaries 19

   Theme 1: Silly Stories

   Dragon Gets By 21

   Julius 22

   Mrs. Brown Went to Town 23

   Theme 2: Nature Walk

   Henry and Mudge and the Starry Night 24

   Exploring Parks with Ranger Dockett 25

   Around the Pond: Who's Been Here? 26

   Theme 3: Around Town:

      Neighborhood and Community

   Chinatown 27

   A Trip to the Firehouse 28

   Big Bushy Mustache 29

   Jamaica Louise James 30

   Theme 4: Amazing Animals

   Officer Buckle and Gloria 31

   Ant 32

   The Great Ball Game 33

   Theme 5: Family Time

   Brothers and Sisters 34

   Jalapeño Bagels 35

   Carousel .36

   Thunder Cake 37

   Theme 6: Talent Show

   The Art Lesson 38

   Moses Goes to a Concert 39

   The School Mural 40

Assignment Cards 43

   Theme 1: Silly Stories

   Dragon Gets By 43

   Julius 45

   Mrs. Brown Went to Town 47

   Theme 2: Nature Walk

   Henry and Mudge and the Starry Night 49

   Exploring Parks with Ranger Dockett 51

   Around the Pond: Who's Been Here? 53

   Theme 3: Around Town:

      Neighborhood and Community

   Chinatown 55

   A Trip to the Firehouse 57

   Big Bushy Mustache 59

   Jamaica Louise James 61

   Theme 4: Amazing Animals

   Officer Buckle and Gloria 63

   Ant 65

   The Great Ball Game 67

   Theme 5: Family Time

   Brothers and Sisters 69

   Jalapeño Bagels 71

   Carousel .73

   Thunder Cake 75

   Theme 6: Talent Show

   The Art Lesson 77

   Moses Goes to a Concert 79

   The School Mural 81

Observation Checklists 83

Theme 1: Silly Stories 85
Theme 2: Nature Walk 87
Theme 3: Around Town:
   Neighborhood and Community 89
Theme 4: Amazing Animals 91
Theme 5: Family Time 93
Theme 6: Talent Show 95

Selection Tests 109

Theme 1: Silly Stories
Dragon Gets By 99
Julius 101
Mrs. Brown Went to Town 103

Theme 2: Nature Walk
Henry and Mudge and the Starry Night 105
Exploring Parks with Ranger Dockett 107
Around the Pond: Who's Been Here? 109

Theme 3: Around Town:
Neighborhood and Community
Chinatown 111
A Trip to the Firehouse 113
Big Bushy Mustache 115
Jamaica Louise James 117

Theme 4: Amazing Animals
Officer Buckle and Gloria 119
Ant 121
The Great Ball Game 123

Theme 5: Family Time
Brothers and Sisters 125
Jalapeño Bagels 127
Carousel 129
Thunder Cake 131

Theme 6: Talent Show
The Art Lesson 133
Moses Goes to a Concert 135
The School Mural 137

Answer Keys 139
Theme 1: Silly Stories 139
Theme 2: Nature Walk 140
Theme 3: Around Town:
   Neighborhood and Community 141
Theme 4: Amazing Animals 142
Theme 5: Family Time 143
Theme 6: Talent Show 144

Routine Cards 145

Newsletters

Dear Family,

WELCOME...to the new school year.

I'd like to invite you to join me in making this an exciting and rewarding year for your child. One of the things I'll be asking you to do is share information that will help me get to know your child better.

Throughout the year, I'll be sending home ideas for activities that you can do with your child to reinforce what we're learning in school. Please become involved as much as you can. Studies have shown that children who get support at home in reading and learning do better in school.

Here are two suggestions for things to do at home:

- **Read and discuss books with your child.** Even after children have learned to read on their own, there are many benefits to reading aloud to your child—and to letting your child read to you. Visit the library together so you can choose books that both of you will enjoy.

- **Let your child see *you* reading.** It's important to show your child that you think reading is valuable and enjoyable.

One other thing: I always appreciate having adult volunteers assist with classroom activities. If you can give some time in the classroom or at home with preparation, please let me know.

Thanks for working with me as a partner in your child's education. Together, we can help your child have a successful year!

Sincerely,

_____

Estimada familia:

¡Bienvenidos al nuevo año escolar!

Mi deseo es que juntos podamos hacer de éste un año productivo y divertido. Una de las cosas que les voy a pedir es que compartan conmigo información acerca de su niño o niña. Esa información me ayudará a conocer mejor a los niños.

Durante el año escolar, les enviaré cartas con ideas de actividades que pueden hacer juntos en casa. Esas actividades ayudarán a complementar lo que aprendemos en clase. Por favor, colaboren tanto como puedan. Estudios han demostrado que los niños que reciben apoyo en sus casas siguen mejor en la escuela.

A continuación hay dos sugerencias importantes de actividades que

- **Lean libros juntos y hablen de lo que leen.** Aunque los niños ya sepan leer, es muy beneficioso que usted les lea en voz alta y también que ellos lean en voz alta para los demás. Vayan a la biblioteca y escojan libros que les gusten a ambos.

- **Asegúrense de que su niño o niña lo vea leer a usted.** Es importante que usted demuestre que la lectura es importante y divertida.

Otra cosa importante: Yo siempre aprecio la ayuda que puedan prestar voluntarios adultos con las actividades de la clase. Por favor, avísenme si me pueden ayudar en el salón de clases, o en su casa, con detalles relacionados a la preparación de actividades.

Les agrádezco de antemano por participar en la educación de su niño o niña. Juntos podemos ayudarle a tener un año muy exitoso.

Atentamente,

_____

Newsletter

Silly Stories

Dear Family,

For the next few weeks, we will be enjoying the theme *Silly Stories*. We will be doing plenty of giggling as we read stories about a dragon that shops, a cool pig from Alaska, and farm animals that play house.

Theme-Related Activities to Do Together

Where's Your Funny Bone?

Talk with your child about what makes him or her laugh. Funny noises? Funny pictures? Being tickled? Try to make your child laugh, then challenge him or her to make you laugh.

Attention All Shoppers

Take your child grocery shopping with you. As you make your selections, help your child determine the food group to which an item belongs. Help him or her discover, for example, that yogurt is a dairy product, spinach is a vegetable, and apples are fruit.

Unexpected Guest

Create a story with your child, aloud or on paper. Think of an animal that comes for a visit and stays to cause some mischief. Imagine and discuss what kind of mischief the animal might get into in the kitchen, the bathroom, or other rooms of the house.

Theme-Related Books to Enjoy Together!

If You Give a Moose a Muffin *by Laura Numeroff. Harper 1991 (32p) also paper* When a boy gives a moose a muffin, it sets off a funny chain of events. Available in Spanish as *Si le das un panecillo a un alce.*

The Old Man and His Door *by Gary Soto. Putnam 1996 (32p)* In a humorous mix-up, an old man takes his front door, instead of a pig, to a barbecue.

Tops and Bottoms *by Janet Stevens. Harcourt 1995 (32p)* A clever hare outwits a lazy bear in this trickster tale, a Caldecott Honor book.

Amelia Bedelia *by Peggy Parish. Harper 1992 (64p) also paper* The literal-minded housekeeper keeps things in an uproar with her funny misinterpretations of instructions. Available in Spanish as *Amelia Bedelia.*

Green Eggs and Ham *by Dr. Seuss. Random 1960 (64p) also paper* Sam-I-Am tries to persuade another Seussian character to eat a plate of green eggs and ham. Available in Spanish as *Huevos verdes con jamón.*

All Of Our Noses Are Here *by Alvin Schwartz. Harper 1985 (64p) also paper* The oh-so-silly Brown family stars in five funny tales based on noodle folklore.

Boletín

Cuentos cómicos

Estimada familia:

Durante las próximas semanas, vamos a tratar el tema *Cuentos cómicos*. Nos reiremos bastante a medida que leemos historias acerca de un dragón que va de compras, un cerdito de Alaska y animales de granja que pretenden vivir en una casa.

Actividades para hacer juntos

¿Qué te hace reír?

Hable con su niño o niña acerca de lo que le hace reír. ¿Le hace reír sonidos divertidos? ¿Dibujos

Haga reír a su niño o niña y luego rételo a que lo haga reír a usted.

Atención clientes

Vayan juntos al supermercado. A medida que vayan escogiendo lo que van a comprar, ayude a su niño o niña a determinar el grupo

lo que van a comprar.

Huésped inesperado

Inventen una historia con su niño o niña y cuéntenla en voz alta o escríbanla en una hoja de papel. Piensen en un animal que

Libros relacionados al tema que pueden leer juntos

If You Give a Moose a Muffin *por Laura Numeroff. Harper 1991 (32p) disponible como libro de bolsillo* Cuando un niño da un panecillo a un alce, es el comienzo de una cadena de sucesos divertidos. Disponible en español con el título *Si le das un panecillo a un alce.*

The Old Man and His Door *por Gary Soto. Putnam 1996 (32p)* En una equivocación humorística, un señor de edad lleva la puerta del frente de su casa en vez de un puerco a un asado.

Tops and Bottoms *por Janet Stevens. Harcourt 1995 (32p)* Este libro que recibió honores de Caldecott, cuenta la historia tradicional de una liebre astuta que le sale adelante a un oso perezoso.

Amelia Bedelia *por Peggy Parish. Harper 1992 (64p) disponible como libro de bolsillo* Amelia Bedelia sigue las cosas muy al pie de la letra. Disponible en español con el título *Amelia Bedelia.*

Green Eggs and Ham *por Dr. Seuss. Random 1960 (64p) disponible como libro de bolsillo* Juan Ramón y su famoso plato de huevos verdes con jamón aparecen en este cuento de verso en rima. Disponible en español con el título *Huevos verdes con jamón.*

All of Our Noses Are Here *por Alvin Schwartz. Harper 1985 (64p) disponible como libro de bolsillo* La muy cómica familia Brown protagonisa estos cinco cuentos divertidos, basados en un cuento tradicional.

Newsletter

Nature Walk

Dear Family,

During the next few weeks, we will be investigating the theme *Nature Walk*. We will learn about camping in the woods, take a walk through a city park with a park ranger, and discover animals that live in and around a pond.

Theme-Related Activities to Do Together

Animal Tracks
Help your child discover animal clues. Help look for tracks, empty nests, or a hole in the ground where an animal may have burrowed. Ask, What animal may have been here? and What makes you think that?

Camp Out at Home
Set up camp with your child at home. Use chairs and a blanket to construct a tent. Pack a snack, head for the great indoors and tell stories around an imaginary camp fire.

What Lives There ?
Ask your child what habitat he or she would like to learn more about. Visit the library to discover what the habitat is like. Make a list of animals that live in that habitat.

Theme-Related Books to Enjoy Together!

Secret Place by *Eve Bunting. Clarion 1996 (32p)* In the middle of a city, a boy finds a place where ducks nest and possums come to drink.

Miss Rumphius by *Barbara Cooney. Viking 1982 (32p) also paper* Miss Rumphius makes her community a more beautiful place by planting lupines. Available in Spanish as *La señorita Runfio.*

Owl Moon by *Jane Yolen. Philomel 1987 (32p)* In a Caldecott Award story, a father and daughter go owling in the woods on a winter's evening.

Bringing the Rain to Kapiti Plain by *Verna Aardema. Dial 1981 (32p) also paper* In a cumulative African tale, Ki-Pat brings rain to drought-stricken Kapiti Plain.

Ant Cities by *Arthur Dorros. Harper 1988 (32p) also paper* Each ant that lives in a hill has a special job, whether it is cleaning the nest or gathering food. Available in Spanish as *Ciudades de hormigas.*

Desert Babies by *Kathy Darling. Walker 1997 (32p)* An introduction to the baby animals that make their home in various deserts.

Boletín

Vamos afuera

Estimada familia:

Durante las próximas semanas, vamos a investigar el tema *Vamos afuera*. También vamos a aprender acerca de acampar en el bosque, vamos a dar una caminata con un guardabosques en un parque de la ciudad y a descubrir animales que viven en una charca y en sus alrededores.

Actividades para hacer juntos

Huellas de animales

Ayude a su niño o niña a descubrir claves de animales que han estado cerca. Ayúdele a buscar huellas, nidos vacíos o un hueco en la tierra, en donde un animal se pudo haber escondido.

Acampar en casa

Hagan juntos un campamento en casa. Usen asientos y mantas para construir la carpa. Preparen comida ligera para acampar, entren a la carpa y cuenten historias alrededor de una hoguera imaginaria.

¿Qué vive allí?

Pregunte a su niño o niña acerca de qué medio ambiente le gustaría aprender más: un lago, un bosque, un desierto o un océano. Visite la biblioteca para aprender más acerca del medio ambiente que escogieron.

Libros relacionados al tema que pueden leer juntos

Secret Place *por Eve Bunting. Clarion 1996 (32p)* En plena ciudad, un niño encuentra un lugar donde los patos ponen sus nidos y en donde las zarigüeyas toman agua.

Miss Rumphius *por Barbara Cooney. Viking 1982 (32p) disponible como libro de bolsillo* La señorita Rumphius siembra lupinos y así hace de su comunidad un lugar más hermoso. Disponible en español con el título *La señorita Runfio.*

Owl Moon *por Jane Yolen. Philomel 1987 (32p)* Esta historia que recibió el premio Caldecott, cuenta la historia de un padre y su hija que van al bosque en una noche de invierno.

Bringing the Rain to Kapiti Plain *por Verna Aardema. Dial 1981 (32p) disponible como libro de bolsillo* En un cuento africano, Ki-pat trae lluvia a la seca llanura de Kapiti.

Ant Cities *por Arthur Dorros. Harper 1988 (32p) disponible como libro de bolsillo* Todas las hormigas tienen una función específica, desde limpiar el nido hasta ir en busca de comida. Disponible en español con el título *Ciudades de hormigas.*

Desert Babies *por Kathy Darling. Walker 1997 (32p)* Esta es una introducción a los animales jóvenes que hacen sus viviendas en diferentes desiertos.

Newsletter

Dear Family,

During the next few weeks, we will be exploring the theme *Around Town: Neighborhood and Community*. As we read, we will investigate different neighborhoods and learn about some of the people who live and work in them.

Around Town:

Neighborhood and Community

Theme-Related Activities to Do Together

Read This Sign

While out in the community with your child, point out to each other the different signs you see. Are they different sizes? Why are some words or numbers on a sign bigger than other words on the same sign? As you help your child read signs, compare and contrast them.

Make a Survey

Make a five-minute survey with your child of the different ways people travel in your neighborhood. How many people do you see walking? Driving? In-line skating? Riding on a bus or train? Record your findings on a chart.

All in the Community

As you do errands with your child, talk about different jobs that help your community. For instance, you might point out park rangers, firefighters, or shop owners. Start a discussion about the jobs by asking your child what they think a particular job is like.

Theme-Related Books to Enjoy Together!

The Paperboy by Dav Pilkey. Orchard 1996 (32p) Early in the morning, a boy and his dog deliver newspapers in this Caldecott Honor book.

I Know a Lady by Charlotte Zolotow. Greenwillow 1984 (32p) also paper A girl tells how an elderly woman in her neighborhood makes all the children feel special. Available in Spanish as *Mi amiga la señora mayor.*

Good-bye Curtis by Kevin Henkes. Greenwillow 1995 (32p) A group of neighbors surprise their letter carrier with a special party on the day of his retirement.

Isla by Arthur Dorros. Dutton 1995 (32p) also paper A girl and her grandmother take an imaginary trip to the Caribbean island where the grandmother grew up. Available in Spanish as *La isla.*

Yoshi's Feast by Kimiko Kajikawa. DK Ink 2000 (32p) Two neighbors find a profitable way to solve a dispute in this folktale.

Rush Hour by Christine Loomis. Houghton 1996 (32p) Rhyming verse describes people in the city rushing to work and then home again.

Boletín

Estimada familia:

Durante las próximas semanas, vamos a tratar el tema *Vivimos aquí*. A medida que leemos, vamos a explorar distintos vecindarios y a aprender acerca de las personas que viven y trabajan en ellos.

Actividades para hacer juntos

Lee la señal

Mientras paseen juntos por su comunidad, indiquen ambos las distinas señales que vean. Luego compárenlas y contrástenlas. ¿Hay señales de distintos tamaños? ¿Por qué hay palabras o números más grandes que otros en la misma señal?

Hagan una encuesta

Hagan juntos una encuesta de las distintas maneras en que las personas se transportan en su vecindario. ¿Cuántas personas ven caminando? ¿conduciendo? ¿en patines? ¿Cuántas viajan en autobús o en tren? Anoten los resultados en una tabla.

En comunidad

Mientras hace mandados con su niño o niña, hablen de los diferentes trabajos que ayudan a su comunidad. Para comenzar la conversación, pregunte en lo que él o ella cree que consiste un trabajo en particular.

Libros relacionados al tema que pueden leer juntos

The Paperboy *por Dav Pilkey. Orchard 1996 (32p)* En este libro que recibió honores de Caldecott, un niño y su perro reparten periódicos temprano en la mañana.

I Know a Lady *por Charlotte Zolotow. Greenwillow 1984 (32p) disponible como libro de bolsillo* Una niña cuenta la historia de una señora mayor en su vecindario que hace que todos los niños se sientan especiales. Disponible en español con el título *Mi amiga la señora mayor.*

Good-bye Curtis *por Kevin Henkes. Greenwillow 1995 (32p)* Los habitantes de un vecindario sorprenden al cartero con una fiesta para el día de su jubilación.

Isla *por Arthur Dorros. Dutton 1995 (32p) disponible como libro de bolsillo* Una niña y su abuela hacen un viaje imaginario a la isla del Caribe en donde creció la abuela. Disponible en español con el título *La isla.*

Yoshi's Feast *por Kimiko Kajikawa. DK Ink 2000 (32p)* En este cuento tradicional, dos vecinos descubren una manera lucrativa de resolver una disputa.

Rush Hour *por Christine Loomis. Houghton 1996 (32p)* Esta selección de verso en rima describe como los trabajadores en una ciudad se apresuran para ir al trabajo y volver a sus casas.

Newsletter

Dear Family,

During the next few weeks, we will be enjoying the theme *Amazing Animals*. We will read about some incredible and hilarious animals: a dog that gives safety tips, ants that build colonies, and a bat that plays lacrosse!

Amazing Animals

Theme-Related Activities to Do Together

Fur, Feather, and Scales

Help your child become a good observer. Whether you see animals in the neighborhood, or look at them in a book, ask your child to tell you about how the animals are alike and different.

What's *That*?

Create an imaginary animal with your child, and then draw or construct it. Questions to help you get started could be: What does it look like?, What does it eat?, How does it move?, and What kind of sound does it make? Don't forget to name your creation!

Guess What I Am

Play animal charades with your child. Mimic different animals and the way they walk, how they get their food, and even how they sound. Take turns guessing and mimicking.

Theme-Related Books to Enjoy Together!

Doctor DeSoto *by William Steig. Farrar 1982 (32p) also paper* A mouse dentist and his wife outwit a fox that wants to eat them in this Caldecott Honor story. Available in Spanish as *Doctor de Soto*.

Coyote *by Gerald McDermott. Harcourt (32p) also paper* Coyote persuades some crows to help him fly in this Native American trickster tale. Available in Spanish as *Coyote*.

Buddy: The First Seeing Eye Dog *by Eva Moore. Scholastic 1996 (48p) also paper* A true account of the German shepherd that became famous as the first seeing-eye dog in America.

Puss in Boots *by Fred Marcellino. Farrar 1990 (32p) also paper* A clever cat gains a fortune for his master in this fairy tale. Available in Spanish as *El gato con botas*.

Biggest, Strongest, Fastest *by Steve Jenkins. Houghton 1995 (32p) also paper* Fun facts about the fastest runner and other record holders of the animal world.

Chameleon *by Rebecca Stefoff. Benchmark 1996 (32p)* The amazing chameleon can change colors faster than you can count to ten.

Boletín

Estimada familia:

Durante las próximas semanas, vamos a tratar el tema *Animales asombrosos*. Vamos a leer acerca de animales increíbles y divertidos: un perro que da consejos de seguridad, hormigas que forman colonias y un murciélago que juega lacrosse.

Animales asombrosos

Actividades para hacer juntos

Piel, plumas y escamas

Ayude a su niño o niña a convertirse en un buen observador. Sin importar si los animales que usted mencione son reales o si los ve en un libro, pida a su niño o niña que le diga en qué se parecen y en qué se diferencian los animales.

¿Qué es eso?

Construyan o dibujen juntos un animal imaginario. Algunas preguntas que se podrían hacer para comenzar pueden incluir: ¿Cómo es su apariencia física? ¿Qué come? ¿Qué tipo de sonidos hace? No se olviden de nombrar su creación.

Adivina qué soy

Jueguen juntos a adivinar a quién imitan. Imiten la manera en que distintos animales caminan, comen y suenan. Cambien de papel en cada turno, de manera que uno haga la imitación mientras el otro trata de adivinar.

Libros relacionados al tema que pueden leer juntos

Doctor DeSoto *por William Steig. Farrar 1982 (32p) disponible como libro de bolsillo* En este libro que recibió honores de Caldecott, un ratoncito dentista y su esposa le salen adelante a un zorro que se los quiere comer. Disponible en español con el título *Doctor de Soto*.

Coyote *por Gerald McDermott. Harcourt (32p) disponible como libro de bolsillo* En este cuento indigenista, Coyote persuade a algunos cuervos a que le ayuden a volar. Disponible en español con el título *Coyote*.

Buddy: The First Seeing Eye Dog *por Eva Moore. Scholastic 1996 (48p) disponible como libro de bolsillo* Una versión verídica del pastor alemán que se volvió famoso por ser el primer perro lazarillo, o guía de ciegos, en los Estados Unidos.

Puss in Boots *por Fred Marcellino. Farrar 1990 (32p) disponible como libro de bolsillo* En este cuento de hadas, un gato ingenioso gana una fortuna para su dueño. Disponible en español con el título *El gato con botas*.

Biggest, Strongest, Fastest *por Steve Jenkins. Houghton 1995 (32p) disponible como libro de bolsillo* Información acerca del animal más veloz y de otros animales que baten récords en el reino animal.

Chameleon *por Rebecca Stefoff. Benchmark 1996 (32p)* El increíble camaleón puede cambiar de colores más rápido de lo que usted puede contar hasta diez.

Newsletter

Dear Family,

During the next few weeks, we will be exploring the theme *Family Time*. We will read stories about brothers and sisters, a family business, a special birthday present, and a young girl who is afraid of thunderstorms. Along the way, we will discover how people in families learn from and help one another.

Theme-Related Activities to Do Together

Family Tree
Create a family tree with your child. Make a list of the names of your family members. Names can be represented by different leaves or branches. You might also wish to make a family garden in which every name is represented by a different flower.

Around the World
Discuss your family background with your child. Help your child find where you live on a map, and where other family members live or have lived. Talk about the traditions, customs, and food that are part of your family.

Tall, Taller, Tallest
Construct a height chart with your child. Make lines on paper attached to the wall to show everyone's height. Help your child to keep track monthly.

Theme-Related Books to Enjoy Together!

Abuela *by Arthur Dorros. Dutton 1991 (32p) also paper* A girl and her grandmother take an imaginary flight over their city. Available in Spanish as *Abuela*.

A Chair for My Mother *by Vera B. Williams. Greenwillow 1988 (32p) also paper* A girl and her mother save their money to buy a comfortable armchair. Available in Spanish as *Un sillón para mi mamá*.

Families *by Ann Morris. Harper 2000 (32p)* A brief photo-essay celebrates families all around the world.

Alexander and the Terrible, Horrible, No Good, Very Bad Day *by Judith Viorst. Simon 1972 (32p) also paper* Alexander knows it's going to be a bad day when he wakes up with gum in his hair. Available in Spanish as *Alexander y el día terrible, horrible, espantoso, horroroso*.

The Riddle Streak *by Susan Beth Pfeffer. Holt 1993 (32p) also paper* Amy learns riddles in the hope of besting her brother at something.

Henry and Mudge in the Family Trees *by Cynthia Rylant. Simon 1997 (40p)* Henry and his dog Mudge have more fun than they thought they would at a family reunion.

Boletín

Estimada familia:

Durante las próximas semanas, vamos a explorar el tema *En familia*. Vamos a leer historias acerca de hermanos y hermanas, de un negocio de familia, de un regalo especial de cumpleaños y de una niña que le teme a las tormentas.

Actividades para hacer juntos

Árbol genealógico

Hagan juntos un árbol geneológico de su familia. Preparen una lista con los nombres de los miembros de la familia. Los nombres se pueden poner en diferentes ramas del árbol.

Alrededor del mundo

Hablen juntos de la historia de su familia. Ayude a su niño o niña a localizar en un mapa la ciudad en donde viven y los lugares donde viven otros familiares. Hablen de las tradiciones, costumbres y comidas que forman parte de su familia.

Alto, más alto, el más alto

Hagan juntos una regla para medir estaturas. Peguen un hoja larga en una pared y cada vez que midan a alguien, dibujen una raya con su nombre. Ayude a su niño o niña a medir las estaturas una vez al mes.

Libros relacionados al tema que pueden leer juntos

Abuela *por Arthur Dorros. Dutton 1991 (32p) disponible como libro de bolsillo* Una niña y su abuela toman un vuelo imaginario por la ciudad. Disponible en español con el título *Abuela*.

A Chair for My Mother *por Vera B. Williams. Greenwillow 1988 (32p) disponible como libro de bolsillo* Una niña y su madre ahorran dinero para comprar un sillón. Disponible en español con el título *Un sillón para mi mamá*.

Families *por Ann Morris. Harper 2000 (32p)* Esta breve colección de fotos es una celebración de familias de todo el mundo.

Alexander and the Terrible, Horrible, No Good, Very Bad Day *por Judith Viorst. Simon 1972 (32p) disponible como libro de bolsillo* Alexander sabe que no va a ser un buen día cuando se despierta y se da cuenta de que tiene goma de mascar pegada en el pelo. Disponible en español con el título *Alexander y el día terrible, horrible, espantoso, horroroso*.

The Riddle Streak *por Susan Beth Pfeffer. Holt 1993 (32p) disponible como libro de bolsillo* Amy aprende adivinanzas para tratar de ser mejor que su hermano en algo.

Henry and Mudge in the Family Trees *por Cynthia Rylant. Simon 1997 (40p)* Henry y su perro Mudge se divierten más de lo esperado en una reunión de la familia.

Newsletter

Dear Family,

Over the next few weeks, we will be enjoying the theme *Talent Show*. We will read stories about a boy who decides to become an artist, a group of schoolchildren who go to a concert, and a class that works on a mural.

Talent Show

Theme-Related Activities to Do Together

Mural

Design and create a mural with your child. Find a blank space on a wall that could use a little color. Measure the space and use paper or cardboard to cover it. Encourage your child to use unusual colors and even attach three-dimensional objects to your mural.

Practice Makes Perfect

Help your child identify something you would both like to learn to do or become better at. Perhaps you'd like to experiment with baking bread, or improve your singing. Work together and talk about what you both do well, and what you would like to improve.

S Is for Smiles

With your child, create an acrostic poem using his or her name. Use each letter of your child's name as the beginning letter of a phrase. For example, the opening of a poem for the name "David" might be "**D** is for *delightful,* **A** is for *animal lover.*"

Theme-Related Books to Enjoy Together!

The Amazing Bone *by William Steig. Farrar 1984 (32p) also paper* Pearl the pig and her talking bone outwit a band of robbers and a hungry fox. Available in Spanish as *El hueso prodigioso.*

The Upside Down Boy *by Juan Felipe Herrera. Children's Book 2000 (32p)* The author's teacher and family help him find his voice through poetry, art, and music. Text in English and Spanish.

Music, Music for Everyone *by Vera Williams. Greenwillow 1984 (32p) also paper* To raise money to help her mother, Rosa and her friends form the Oak Street Band.

Dance *by Bill T. Jones and Susan Kuklin. Hyperion 1999 (32p)* Photos and spare text present the gifted dancer Jones in fluid movement across the pages.

The Legend of the Indian Paintbrush *by Tomie dePaola. Putnam 1988 (32p) also paper* Little Gopher looks for a way to paint the colors of the sunset. Available in Spanish as *Leyenda del pincel indio.*

Song and Dance Man *by Karen Ackerman. Knopf 1988 (32p) also paper* Grandpa puts on an entertaining vaudeville show for his three grandchildren.

Boletín

¡Aplausos!

Estimada familia:

Durante las próximas semanas, vamos a tratar el tema *¡Aplausos!* Vamos a leer historias acerca de un niño que decide volverse artista, de una clase escolar que hace un mural y de un grupo que va a un concierto.

Actividades para hacer juntos

Mural

Diseñen y hagan un mural juntos. Busquen una pared o parte de una pared a la que le falte un poco de color. Mida el espacio en que van a trabajar y cúbranlo con cartulina. Anime a su niño a usar colores inusuales y a que pegue objetos a su mural.

La práctica hace al maestro

Identifiquen juntos algo que a ambos les gustaría aprender o algo que les gustaría poder hacer mejor. Trabajen juntos y hablen de cosas que hacen bien y de cosas que les gustaría poder hacer mejor.

La S de sonrisa

Escriban juntos un poema "acróstico" con el nombre de su niño o niña. En un poema acróstico, cada letra del nombre es el comienzo de una frase. Por ejemplo, el comienzo del poema para el nombre "David" podría ser: "**D** es por lo *digno*, **A** es por la manera en que *actúa*."

Libros relacionados al tema que pueden leer juntos

The Amazing Bone *por William Steig. Farrar 1984 (32p) disponible como libro de bolsillo* Una cerdita y su hueso prodigioso le salen adelante a una banda de ladrones y un zorro hambriento. Disponible en español con el título *El hueso prodigioso*.

The Upside Down Boy *Por Juan Felipe Herrera. Children's Book 2000 (32p)* El maestro la familia del autor le ayudan a hallar su voz en la poesía, el arte y la música. El texto del libro es en inglés y español.

Music, Music for Everyone *por Vera Williams. Greenwillow 1984 (32p) disponible como libro de bolsillo* Para recaudar dinero para ayudar a su madre, Rosa y sus amigos forman la banda musical Oak Street Band.

Dance *por Bill T. Jones and Susan Kuklin. Hyperion 1999 (32p)* Una combinación de fotos y texto representan los movimientos fluidos del talentoso bailarín Jones.

The Legend of the Indian Paintbrush *por Tomie dePaola. Putnam 1988 (32p) disponible como libro de bolsillo* Pequeño Topo busca una manera de pintar los colores de la puesta del sol. Disponible en español con el título *Leyenda del pincel indio*.

Song and Dance Man *por Karen Ackerman. Knopf 1988 (32p) disponible como libro de bolsillo* El abuelo realiza una función de variedades muy entretenida para sus tres nietos.

Selection Summaries

Dragon Gets By

Dragon was out of food, and he was very **hungry.** He went to the store to buy some food. The store was on top of a hill.

Dragon got a lot of food and put it all in his cart. He had so much food that he could not fit it all into his car. What could he do?

Dragon had an idea. He would eat some of the food. Then he could fit the rest in his car. He sat down and ate. He kept eating and eating. Soon, all of the food was gone. But now Dragon did not fit into his little car!

Dragon had to push his car home. The car rolled down the hill. It rolled very fast, and he could not keep up. At last, Dragon's car stopped in front of his house.

All of this running made Dragon hungry. But he still did not have any food in his house.

"Time to go **shopping**," said Dragon.

Julius

Maya's granddaddy came to Maya's house with a big box. It was a gift for Maya. Maya hoped it was a big brother or a horse. But it was a pig. His name was Julius.

At first, Maya's mom and dad did not like Julius. He was messy. He ate a lot of food and left **crumbs** on the sheets. He made a lot of **noise**.

But Julius loved Maya. Julius and Maya had a lot of fun together. They liked to try on hats, swing for hours, and eat peanut butter together. Julius taught Maya how to dance. And Maya showed Julius how to be nice.

Julius tried not to be messy. Maya's mom and dad liked that. They started to like having Julius in their house. And that was a good thing, because Julius and Maya were best friends.

Mrs. Brown Went to Town

Mrs. Brown lived on a farm with a cow, two pigs, three ducks, and a yak. One day, Mrs. Brown rode her bike into town. A little dog bit her foot.

Mrs. Brown had to go to the hospital. She wrote a note to the cow, two pigs, three ducks and the yak. "Be good," she said in the note.

When the animals got the note, they had an idea. They voted to move into Mrs. Brown's house. They tried **wearing** her clothes. They jumped on her bed. They painted her house red. They ate all of the food in the house. At the end of the day, they all took showers and went to sleep in Mrs. Brown's bed.

That night, Mrs. Brown was **released** from the hospital. She got into bed. She did not see the cow, two pigs, three ducks, and the yak sleeping there. The bed crashed through the floor! Now everyone had to go to the hospital!

After a few days, Mrs. Brown and the animals went home. But now, Mrs. Brown lives in the barn with the cow, two pigs, three ducks and the yak!

Henry and Mudge and the Starry Night

Henry and his big dog, Mudge went on a **camping** trip with Henry's mom and dad. Henry and Mudge loved camping. This summer, they would go to Big Bear Lake.

Henry hoped they would see deer and raccoons. He also hoped they would not see a bear. He was scared of bears. "No bear will get us, Mudge," said Henry.

When they got to Big Bear Lake, everyone went for a **hike**. It was a long walk. Henry saw a fish jump out of the water. He saw a baby deer. He saw a rainbow. Mudge did not see much. He was too busy smelling.

After the hike, Henry's mom set up the **tent**. When it got dark, they all sat by the fire and looked at the stars. Henry had never seen so many stars. Mudge did not look at the stars. He was busy chewing a log.

At last, they all fell asleep under the stars. Henry and Mudge loved camping.

Exploring Parks with Ranger Dockett

Ranger Dockett is a park **ranger**. A park ranger is a person who takes care of a park. Ranger Dockett's park is in the middle of a big city.

Ranger Dockett gives **tours** of the parks. He shows people the plants and animals that live in the park. He makes sure that everyone follows the park rules.

Sometimes Ranger Dockett teaches class at the pond. He goes into the pond with a net. He shows some children a snail that he found in the mud.

Ranger Dockett went to school to learn how to be a ranger. He likes his job. He likes to teach people how to keep the park safe and clean.

Around the Pond: Who's Been Here?

William and Cammy went for a walk with their dog, Sam, around a pond. They were looking for blueberries.

They followed an old deer **path** around the pond. What kinds of animals live around a pond? William and Cammy looked for clues to find out.

They saw a footprint near some soft **moss**. "Who's been here?" they asked. It was a baby raccoon.

They saw a pile of sticks and mud by the **edge** of the pond. "Who's been here?" they asked. It was a beaver.

They found some broken shells. "Who's been here?" they asked. It was an otter.

Cammy and William saw two pails of blueberries. "Who's been here?" they asked. They knew who it was this time! Their parents had been there.

"Come and join us," called their father. And in they went for a swim.

Chinatown

Every morning a boy and his grandmother go for a walk through Chinatown. The boy lives in an **apartment** in Chinatown with his mother, father, and grandmother.

"Watch out for cars, Grandma," he tells her. They see people in the park. They always stop and say hello to Mr. Wong. He fixes shoes.

Every day the boy and his grandma visit shops and walk past **restaurants**. They like to go for lunch together. The boy likes to watch fish swim in the tank at the restaurant.

They go to an outdoor **market** to buy food for dinner. Grandma buys some fresh crabs.

The streets are full of people when it is time for Chinese New Year. "Be sure to stay close by," Grandma tells the boy. The boy and his grandma watch the New Year's parade. Next year he will march too. He tells his grandma to have a happy new year.

"And a happy new year to you too," she says.

A Trip to the Firehouse

David and his class are visiting a firehouse. The fire **chief** greets them at the door. Next they meet the firehouse dog. They go inside the firehouse to feed the dog.

David sees **gear** hanging on the wall. The **firefighters** show how long it takes them to put on their gear. Less than thirty seconds!

A firefighter shows the children how to use the firehouse pole. Whoosh! He slides down the pole.

Next they go to the **dispatch** room. Things are never slow there! When there is an **emergency**, calls come in to the dispatch room. Alarms also come in to the dispatch room.

The children get a good look at a fire truck. They see the bell that clangs and the siren that screams. They help the firefighters wash the truck. Then they go inside the firehouse for a treat.

Clang! Clang! The alarm rings. The firefighters rush out of the room. Off they go down the street. The children watch out the window. They wave to the firefighters. Their visit to the firehouse is over.

Big Bushy Mustache

One morning Ricky's teacher told the class about a school play. "Do you want to wear this white shirt?" she asked Ricky. Ricky shook his head no. When she took out a big **mustache**, Ricky nodded yes.

Ricky played with his mustache all day. When school was over, the teacher told the class to leave their **costumes** in their desks. Ricky wanted to take the **bushy** mustache home. He wanted to show it to his father.

"Look, Mami," he said to his mother. But Ricky's mother didn't see anything. Ricky had lost the mustache!

After dinner, Ricky tried to make a new mustache. He looked in the **mirror**. It didn't look real. That night he told his father about the mustache.

The next morning, Ricky's mother said "I have a surprise for you." She gave him a big, bushy mustache. It was his father's mustache!

"Thank you," he said to his father.

"That's okay," his father said. "But next time listen to your teacher."

Jamaica Louise James

Everything Jamaica Louise sees is something she wants to draw. At night, she sits with her mother and grandmother and shows them her pictures. On her birthday, Jamaica Louise's mother and grandmother gave her a real paint set.

Jamaica's grammy works in a subway **station**. She leaves for work when it is still dark. All day long people line up at Grammy's **booth**. They buy tokens for the subway **train**. At night, Grammy tells Jamaica about the people she sees at the subway station. Jamaica listens and paints.

One day Jamaica had a cool idea for Grammy's birthday. She and her mother went to the subway station. They put pictures up on the walls. Grammy was surprised! Everyone loved the pictures in the subway station.

"That looks like me!" said a lady in a green hat. And Grammy told everyone about Jamaica Louise James.

Officer Buckle and Gloria

Officer Buckle shared **safety** tips with the students at Napville School. Nobody ever listened. Then one day, Officer Buckle took a dog named Gloria with him when he gave a safety speech. This time the children sat up and looked.

Officer Buckle was surprised. He thought the children liked his safety tips. He did not know they were looking at Gloria. She was acting out the tips behind him. After that, many schools called Officer Buckle and Gloria to give safety speeches.

One day, a TV news team filmed Officer Buckle and Gloria. That night, Officer Buckle saw the news. He saw Gloria acting out his safety tips. He thought the children liked Gloria more than him.

The next day, he let Gloria give the safety tips by herself. She fell asleep. So did the children. After Gloria left, Napville School had a big **accident**.

Officer Buckle got letters about the accident. Then he knew he and Gloria did a good job when they worked as a team. He thought of his best safety tip yet . . . "Always stick with your buddy!"

Ant

Ants live all over the world. If you see one ant, you will see many other ants near it. Ants live and work in groups called colonies. Most ant colonies are in **tunnels** under the ground.

Every ant has two long **antennae** on its head. They are like a nose and fingers all in one. The antennae help the ant find food and then find its way back to its colony.

The queen ant is the mother of all the ants in a colony. Worker ants take care of the queen and of the queen's eggs. They bring food to the colony.

The queen ant's eggs turn into **larvae**. Larvae look like little worms. Later the larvae will turn into ants.

Some ants live in wood. Other ants live in nests in trees. And some ants eat juices that come from other insects. These ants are called farmer ants.

Ants are very strong. A lot of ants working together can beat a big beetle. All ants work together in teams and help each other on big jobs. Ants are a lot like us.

The Great Ball Game

Long ago the Birds and the Animals had an **argument**. "Let us have a ball game," said Crane, the leader of the Birds. "The first side to score a goal will win the argument."

The Birds and the Animals formed two teams. Both sides agreed that the winners could name a **penalty** for the other side. The losers would have to **accept** the penalty.

One animal was left out. It was Bat. Bat had wings and teeth.

"You have wings. You must be a bird," Bear said.

The Birds laughed at Bat. "We don't want you," they told him. So Bear told Bat that he could play with the Animals.

The teams played hard. Every time the Birds got the ball, they flew too high for the Animals to reach. The game was almost over.

Suddenly Bat flew onto the field and stole the ball. None of the Birds could stop him. Bat scored a goal. The Animals had won!

Bat was allowed to name the penalty for the Birds. "You Birds must leave this land for half of each year," Bat said. And that is why the Birds fly south each winter.

Brothers and Sisters

What is it like to have a **newborn** brother or sister? Sometimes having a baby in the family is fun. But sometimes a baby is not so much fun.

Brothers and sisters might have to play by themselves if Mommy is busy taking care of the baby. Or they may be able to help **distract** the baby.

Brothers and sisters can have fun together. An older sister can help her younger sister get ready for school.

You learn to share when you have a sister or brother. Sometimes a brother or sister is your best friend. And sometimes it's hard to be a brother or sister.

Twins are brothers and sisters who are the same age. Some twins look a lot alike, but they aren't exactly alike.

Adopted brothers and sisters came from a different mom and dad. But they are still part of the family.

Grandmothers and grandfathers have brothers and sisters. And even after seventy years, they can still be best friends.

Jalapeño Bagels

"What should I bring to school on Monday for International Day?" Pablo asks his mother.

Pablo's parents own a **bakery**. One Sunday, Pablo helps his parents in the bakery. He is trying to pick a food from his **culture** to bring to school.

Pablo thinks about the foods he likes. Should he bring sweet bread to school? Should he bring pumpkin turnovers? Or maybe chango bars?

Pablo's father calls from the back room. He wants Pablo to help him make bagels. First he makes the **dough** in a metal bowl.

Pablo's mother joins them. They make bagels with red peppers called *jalapeños*. Pablo's parents have a special **recipe** for jalapeño bagels.

"Have you decided what you're going to bring to school?" asks Pablo's mother.

"Jalapeño bagels," he tells his parents. "Because they are a mixture of both of you. Just like me!"

Carousel

Alex was about to have a birthday party, but she wasn't happy. "Where's Daddy?" she **grumbled**.

At dinner, Alex hardly ate. As soon as dinner was over, Alex's aunts put birthday presents on the table. Alex opened the first present. "I have a million pairs of pajamas," she said **grumpily**.

She opened more gifts. Each time she opened a gift, Alex **fussed**.

Alex knew her father wasn't coming home for her birthday. She opened the gift he had sent for her. It was a perfect little carousel.

Alex was still **angry**. Her mother sent her to bed.

Then Alex fell asleep. She dreamed that the carousel animals went hopping out the window. She went out after them.

When Alex woke up, she heard her father talking. She told him she was sorry for breaking the carousel.

"And I'm sorry I missed your birthday," he answered.

Thunder Cake

A big storm was coming. The little girl hid under the bed. She was afraid of the **thunder**.

"Child, you come out from under that bed," her grandma said. Grandma told her they would make a Thunder Cake together.

The girl and her grandmother needed to know how far away the storm was. That way they would know how much time they had to make the Thunder Cake. Grandma showed the little girl how to tell how far away a storm is.

"When you see the **lightning**, start counting . . . real slow. When you hear the thunder, stop counting. That number is how many miles away the storm is."

They went out to find the things to make the cake. First they needed eggs from old Nellie Peck Hen. Then they needed milk from old Kick Cow. The girl was scared. BA-BOOOOOM, **rumbled** the thunder.

Inside the house, they mixed everything together. Grandma told the girl that she was brave. They set the table and ate the Thunder Cake.

"Perfect," Grandma said, "just perfect."

The Art Lesson

Tommy knew he wanted to be an artist when he grew up. Drawing pictures was his favorite thing to do.

Tommy's grown-up twin cousins were in art school. They told Tommy never to **copy** and told him to **practice**, practice, practice.

On his birthday, Tommy's mom and dad gave him a box of sixty-four **crayons**. Tommy brought his crayons to school.

"Everyone must use the same crayons," his teacher said. "SCHOOL CRAYONS!"

Mrs. Bowers, the art teacher, told the class to copy her drawing. Tommy didn't want to copy. And he wanted to use his own crayons.

"If you draw the Pilgrim man and woman and the turkey, you can do your own picture with your own crayons," Mrs. Bowers said.

Tommy did, and then he drew his own pictures. And he still does.

Moses Goes to a Concert

Moses has a new drum. Moses is **deaf**. He can't hear the sounds his drum makes, but he can feel the **vibrations** through his hands and feet.

Moses and his class are going on field trip. They are going to a young people's concert.

Inside, a young woman walks onto the stage. Her name is Marjorie Elwyn. She plays **percussion instruments**, such as the drum.

"She has no shoes!" Moses **signs** to his friends.

"She is deaf, too," his teacher signs.

Then Mr. Samuels takes eleven balloons out of his bag. "Hold them on your laps," signs Mr. Samuels. "They'll help you feel the music."

When the concert is over, Mr. Samuels has a surprise. Ms. Elwyn will let them play her instruments.

That night, Moses tells his parents about the concert. "When you set your mind to it, you can become anything you want," he signs.

The School Mural

"I have some news," Mrs. Sanchez told her class. "Soon our school will be fifty years old."

Mrs. Sanchez told the class to think of a **project**. "It should be about our school and our community," she said.

That day, Mei Lee saw a big painting on a wall. It was a **mural**. "Let's make a mural," she said.

The children in the class took a vote. They voted to make a mural to show their school **pride**.

The children told their families about the mural. For the next three weeks, the class worked on the mural. First, they planned what to draw. Then, the art teacher helped the children draw **sketches**.

When the mural was done, a reporter from the newspaper came to ask the class questions. He took photos of the mural with the painters in front of it.

People came to see the mural. One neighbor thanked the children for making such a beautiful painting. He told the children that people would enjoy their school mural for many years.

Assignment Cards

Reading Routines

Before You Read . . .

- Flip through the pages of the story. Look at the pictures to get an idea of what the story might be about.

While You Read . . .

- **Think of questions** you have about characters and events in the story. Look for answers to your questions as you read the story.

- **Complete your story map**. Fill in the things that happen in the beginning, middle, and end of the story.

Theme 1: Silly Stories

Can a Sleeping Bag Snore?

Play on Words

An author can make a "play on words" by using a word that can have different meanings. On page 20, you can see a funny picture of Dragon's "balanced diet." Think of your own play on words and draw a picture to show the different meanings.

Theme 1: Silly Stories

Literature Discussion

- What makes Dragon a funny character?

- What could you explain to Dragon that might help him think of better solutions to his problems?

- What do you think of the things Dragon bought? What kinds of foods do you think he should have bought?

- Have you ever fixed one problem, but caused a new one?

Theme 1: Silly Stories

Reading Routines

Before You Read . . .

- Flip through the pages of the story. Look at the pictures to see what the story might be about.

While You Read . . .

- **Think of questions** you have about what would happen if a pig went to live with a little girl. Look for answers to your questions as you read the story.

- **Talk to your classmates** about your questions. Listen to their questions, too. Then talk about the answers you find.

Theme 1: Silly Stories

What a Mess!

Making Decisions

With a small group, write a list of messes that Julius might make in Maya's house. Decide together which messes on your list are big and which ones are small.

Make a new list, writing the messes in order from the smallest mess to the biggest mess.

Theme 1: Silly Stories

Literature Discussion

- How would you describe Julius to someone who doesn't know him?

- How did living with a pig change things for Maya's family?

- Do you think it would be fun to live with a pig? Why or why not?

- What would your mother or father do and say if you brought a pig home to live in your house? How would you talk your mother or father into letting you keep the pig?

Theme 1: Silly Stories

Learn Good Manners

Making Lists

Think about manners and what they are for. With a small group, discuss why you think manners are important to learn, or why you think they are not important. Then make a list of manners Maya might teach Julius.

Theme 1: Silly Stories

Reading Routines

Before You Read . . .

- Flip through the pages of the story. Look at the pictures to see what the story might be about.

While You Read . . .

- **Think of questions** you have about characters and events in the story. Talk to your classmates about your questions. Look for answers as you read the story.

- **Complete your Prediction Chart**. Fill in: What Happens in the Story, and What Would Happen If. . . .

Theme 1: Silly Stories

Funny Characters

Using Details to Show Character

An author uses details to tell readers about the characters in a story. Read pages 78 and 79 again. List details that show that the animals like to have fun. The author could have written, "The animals had fun in the house." But you would not have known as much about the animals. List other details you could use to show that the animals like to have fun.

Theme 1: Silly Stories

Literature Discussion

- How are the animals in the story different from other animals?

- What would be fun about playing with the animals when they are in Mrs. Brown's house? What would not be fun about it?

- What do you think would be good and bad about living in the barn with the animals?

Theme 1: Silly Stories

Now It's Time to Make a Rhyme

Rhyming Words

Choose one or two pairs of rhyming words from the story. Use each pair of words in a sentence to make a rhyme. Share your rhymes with a partner or with the class.

Theme 1: Silly Stories

Reading Routines

Before You Read . . .

- Flip through the story to get an idea of what it might be about.

While You Read . . .

- **Think of questions** you have about characters and events in the story. Look for answers to your questions as you read the story. Reread the text if you still need answers to your questions.

- **Talk to your friends** about what you think of Henry's camping trip.

- **Complete your Venn diagram.** Fill it in to show how the characters are alike and different

Theme 2: Nature Walk

Act It Out

Dialogue

Choose a partner. One partner can play the part of Henry, and one can play Mudge. Read Henry's words on pages 138 and 139. Think how Henry is feeling. Is he excited? Is he scared? Does he feel safe with Mudge? Read the words aloud as you think Henry might say them.

Then switch parts and act out the scene again.

Theme 2: Nature Walk

Literature Discussion

- Do you know any dogs like Mudge? Would you like to have Mudge as a pet? Why or why not?

- Would you like to go camping with Henry and his family? Why or why not?

- What clues tell you how Henry feels about this camping trip?

Theme 2: Nature Walk

Draw What You Feel

Mood

Draw a picture that shows how this story makes you feel. Then write the following sentence below the picture, filling in the blanks:

This story makes me feel _____

because _____.

Share your picture, sentence, and feelings with your classmates.

Theme 2: Nature Walk

Reading Routines

Before You Read . . .

- Think about what you know about parks and park rangers. Look at the pictures to see what the job of a park ranger is like.

- Begin your K-W-L Chart. Write what you already know about park rangers. Then write what you want to know about park rangers.

While You Read . . .

- **Reread sentences that are hard.** Look at the pictures again to help you understand the hard sentences.

- **Think of questions** you have about parks and park rangers.

- **Complete your K-W-L Chart.**

Theme 2: Nature Walk

Literature Discussion

- What is your favorite part of Ranger Dockett's job?

- Would you like to be a park ranger? Why?

- Why do you think we need park rangers?

Theme 2: Nature Walk

Are They Alike?

Word Structure

Look at page 177 and reread the last sentence. What is a **habitat**? If you are not sure, look it up in a dictionary.

Now read this word: **inhabit**. The word **inhabit** means "to live in." How are the words **habitat** and **inhabit** alike?

Write a sentence using each word. Share your sentences with a friend.

Theme 2: Nature Walk

Reading Routines

Before You Read . . .

- Think about what you know about ponds. Look at the pictures to get an idea of what the pond in the story is like.

While You Read . . .

- **Reread sentences that are hard.** Look at the pictures again to help you understand the hard sentences.

- **Think about each animal.** Think of ways each animal is the same as or different from other animals in the story.

- **Complete your Around the Pond Chart.** List each animal under Birds, Fish, Mammals, or Reptiles.

Theme 2: Nature Walk

What's Your Favorite?

Favorite Animal

What animal from the story is your favorite? What do you know about this animal from the story?

Look in books and magazines in your classroom to find out more about this animal. Where does it live? What does it eat?

Draw a picture of your favorite animal. Write what you have learned about it.

Theme 2: Nature Walk

Literature Discussion

- What would you like most about taking a walk around the pond with William and Cammy?

- What animal from the story would you most like to see? Why?

Theme 2: Nature Walk

MOOOOVE Over!

Animal Sounds

Make a list of the animals in the story. Think about what you know about how they sound and act. Use books in your classroom to learn more.

Then use what you have learned. Use sounds and actions as you pretend to be each animal.

Theme 2: Nature Walk

Reading Routines

Before You Read . . .

- Flip through the pages to see what kind of neighborhood the story is about.

While You Read . . .

- **Think about the way people live** in Chinatown. Talk to your friends about how this neighborhood is the same as and different from your neighborhood.

- **Look for details** that tell you more about life in Chinatown. Use these details to help you fill in the What I Like Chart.

Theme 3: Around Town: Neighborhood and Community

Literature Discussion

- What are some things you might see if you visited this Chinatown? Which things seem most interesting to you, and why?

- What do you know about the boy in the story from the things that he does?

- Why did the boy and his grandmother hold hands when they crossed the street?

- What kinds of things do you do that let people know you are a good person?

Theme 3: Around Town: Neighborhood and Community

Food for Thought

Restaurant Food

People all over the world like to eat in restaurants.

When you go to a restaurant, what kind of food do you like to eat? Write a paragraph describing the food and tell why you like to eat it.

Share your paragraph with your classmates.

Theme 3: Around Town: Neighborhood and Community

Reading Routines

Before You Read . . .

- Flip through the pages. Predict what you think the story will be about. Discuss your ideas with a classmate.

While You Read . . .

- **Think of questions** you have about the story. Look for answers as you read. Discuss the answers with your classmates.

- **Complete your Details Chart.** Find details in the story that support the main idea. Write the details in the chart.

Theme 3: Around Town: Neighborhood and Community

SPLISH! What's That Sound?

Words That Name Sounds

Read page 303 again. What do you hear? The word *whoosh* makes the sound of a firefighter sliding down the pole.

Words that make sounds are fun to say as you are reading. The words help you hear what is happening.

- Make a list of other words that make sounds you might hear at a firehouse.

- Then think of another place and write some sound words for that place.

Tell what the sound word is describing.

Theme 3: Around Town: Neighborhood and Community

Literature Discussion

- What did you find most interesting about the trip to the firehouse? Why?

- What would you ask the firefighters if you visited them at their firehouse?

- What do you think would be hardest about being a firefighter? What would be easiest? Explain your answers.

- How do firefighters keep themselves safe during a fire?

Theme 3: Around Town: Neighborhood and Community

Reading Routines

Before You Read . . .

- Think about a time when you had a problem. What did you do to solve your problem? What didn't work? Why? What did work? Why?

While You Read . . .

- **Make predictions.** Before you turn each page, think about what might happen next.

- **Complete your Problem-Solving Event Map.** How does Ricky try to solve his problem? Write everything he tries. Then write whether each thing works.

Theme 3: Around Town: Neighborhood and Community

What's He Thinking?

Ricky's Thoughts

The author tells you what Ricky is thinking as he walks home. You find out more about why Ricky likes wearing the mustache. What do you learn about how Ricky feels? How does Ricky feel about his father?

Read page 335 again. Pretend you are Ricky and write just what you are thinking at this point in the story.

Theme 3: Around Town: Neighborhood and Community

Literature Discussion

- Tell about the different feelings Ricky has in the first half of the story. What causes each feeling?

- Do Ricky's feelings and actions remind you of anything that has happened in your life?

- How does Ricky feel when people tell him he looks just like his mother?

Theme 3: Around Town: Neighborhood and Community

That's a Whopper!

Exaggeration

When we exaggerate, we make something seem bigger or more important than it really is.

Your friend might say, "My uncle's car is so big three elephants could fit inside it." You would know that was not true. But you would know that it was a really big car.

An author sometimes exaggerates to make a character's action or feeling seem stronger or more important.

- How does the author exaggerate in the last sentence, page 355?

- Write three exaggerations of your own. Share them with friends.

Theme 3: Around Town: Neighborhood and Community

Reading Routines

Before You Read . . .

- Flip through the pages of the story. The pictures show clues to what happens in the story. The pictures also show clues to how people in the story feel. Look for these clues.

While You Read . . .

- **Think of questions** you have about characters and events in the story. Talk to your classmates about your questions. Then talk about the answers you found.

- **Complete your I Can Use Clues Chart.** Write the clues you find in the words and pictures of the story.

Theme 3: Around Town: Neighborhood and Community

Literature Discussion

- What would you do with a paint set like Jamaica's if you had one?

- Would you like to travel on a subway?
  Why or why not?

- Would you like to have Jamaica as a friend? Why or why not?

Theme 3: Around Town: Neighborhood and Community

Word Choice Winners!

Specific Verbs

Verbs are words that show action. Some verbs are very specific, and some are not.

There are many ways to look. We can peek or we can stare. **Peek** and **stare** are more specific than **look**.

In the story, the author uses the verbs **sneak** and **swoosh**. Make a list of other specific verbs in the story.

If you want to, use some of the verbs in a story of your own. Share your story with a friend.

Theme 3: Around Town: Neighborhood and Community

Let's Make Up a Story

Writing a Story

Think about the people Jamaica includes in her artwork.

- Choose a person from one of Jamaica's paintings, or make up a character of your own.

- Write a story about the person you selected.

Theme 3: Around Town: Neighborhood and Community

Reading Routines

Before You Read . . .

- Flip through the pages of the story. Look at the pictures to get an idea of what the story might be about.

While You Read . . .

- **Think of things that might happen next**. Write them in your journal. See if your guesses are correct.

- **Complete your Drawing Conclusions Chart.** Use what you learn from the story about Officer Buckle, Gloria, the students, and the principal to complete your chart.

Theme 4: Amazing Animals

Let's Play It Safe!

Safety Tips

Think about what helps make your classroom a safe place.

In a group, make a list of safety tips. When you are finished, have someone in your group read your safety tips.

Finally, write each tip on a strip of paper. Then put the strips on the bulletin board.

Theme 4: Amazing Animals

Literature Discussion

- Why do the children sit up and listen everywhere Officer Buckle and Gloria go?

- Does Officer Buckle know how amazing Gloria is? Explain your answer.

- Would you tell Officer Buckle what Gloria does during his safety tips talk? Why or why not?

Theme 4: Amazing Animals

Picture Clues

Character Sketch

Look at page 43 of the story.

The picture has many clues about what kind of person Officer Buckle is. Look closely at the picture.

Make notes about what these things tell you about Officer Buckle. Read your notes to your class.

Theme 4: Amazing Animals

Reading Routines

Before You Read . . .

- What would you like to learn about ants? Write your questions about ants in your journal.

While You Read . . .

- **Write the answers to your questions.** When you find answers to your questions, write them in your journal.

- **Complete your Text Organization Chart.** Write the details that tell more about the main idea.

Theme 4: Amazing Animals

Hear! Hear! Listen to Me!

Kinds of Antennae

Think about an ant's antennae. Write what you know about them.

Then think of other kinds of antennae that you know about. Write about another kind of antenna.

Are the two kinds of antennae alike in any way? Tell how.

Theme 4: Amazing Animals

Literature Discussion

- What are some amazing things about ants?

- Which of these seems most interesting to you, and why?

- In what ways are ants like people?

- What more do you want to learn about ants?

Theme 4: Amazing Animals

What's for Dinner?

What Ants Eat

What do ants eat? How do they get their food?

Look back at the story. Make a list of three ways ants get their food.

Can you add to your list? Look for books or magazines in your classroom that tell more about ants and their food.

Theme 4: Amazing Animals

Reading Routines

Before You Read . . .

- Read the title and look at the picture on the cover. Think about why birds and animals might play against each other in a ball game.

While You Read . . .

- **Write in your journal** how you feel about the argument between the Birds and the Animals. Tell why you do or do not think that playing a ball game is a good way to settle the argument.

Theme 4: Amazing Animals

I'm a Good Team Player

Persuasive Speaking

Imagine that you are Bat. Choose the team that you would like to be on—the Birds or the Animals.

Write a speech that would make the players want you on their team.

Read your speech to your classmates.

Theme 4: Amazing Animals

Literature Discussion

- What would you tell the characters in the story if you could talk to them?

- Do you think a ball game will really show which group is better? Why or why not?

- If you could choose to be on one of the teams, which would you choose? Why?

- How would you help the groups settle their argument?

Theme 4: Amazing Animals

Wow! What a Game!

Play-by-Play Description

Choose a partner. Discuss how the author uses words such as *flew*, *stole*, and *darted* to help you picture the action in the story.

Think of some other interesting action words.

Now, you and your partner can take turns pretending to be sports announcers telling about the ball game between the Birds and the Animals. See how exciting you can make your description using action words.

Theme 4: Amazing Animals

Reading Routines

Before You Read . . .

- Read the title. Then flip through the pages and look at the pictures. Think about what the brothers and sisters might be saying about each other.

While You Read . . .

- **Complete your Generalizations Chart.** Find details from the story that support each generalization in the chart. Write the supporting details in the chart.

Theme 5: Family Time

Times of My Life

Family Scrapbook

Write a list of your favorite experiences in your life. Then write how you felt about each event as it was happening.

Draw pictures of the events or gather photographs, invitations, or other things related to the events.

Make a scrapbook of these special events and share it with your classmates.

Theme 5: Family Time

Literature Discussion

- What are some things that older brothers and sisters liked about having new babies in their families? What are some things they disliked?

- How are your feelings about your brother or sister the same as the feelings of the children in the story? How are your feelings different from theirs?

- What would you say to a friend who is going to have a new brother or sister?

Theme 5: Family Time

Learn Your Roots!

Family Tree

Make a picture of a family tree. Have the branches show the people in your family, starting with you and going back to your great-grandparents, if possible.

Take your family tree home. Have your family help you fill in as many of the branches as possible.

Bring your family tree back to school. Tell what you have learned by making your family tree.

Theme 5: Family Time

Reading Routines

Before You Read . . .

- Read the title of the story and look at the picture on the cover. Think of possible reasons why the boy is standing in the doorway of a bakery.

While You Read . . .

- **Ask questions about Pablo's problem** and the decision he must make. Look for answers as you read the story.

- **Look for details** that help you learn more about the characters. Ask your classmates to tell you which details helped them learn about the characters.

Theme 5: Family Time

Literature Discussion

- Would you enjoy a visit to Pablo's bakery? Why or why not?

- If you were Pablo, how would you decide which treat to take to school for International Day?

- Look at the pictures in the story. How can you tell whether Pablo's family is happy or unhappy about working in the bakery?

Theme 5: Family Time

Delicious Delights!

Describe a Favorite Treat

Pretend that you can buy anything you want at a bakery. Draw a picture of the treat you will buy.

Under your picture, write one sentence to describe the treat. Write another sentence to tell why it is your favorite.

Theme 5: Family Time

Mmmm . . . I'm Hungry!

Writing a Recipe

A recipe tells the ingredients and directions for making a certain food. Look at the recipe on page 211 to see how it's done.

Choose a partner and then pick a kind of sandwich you both like. Together, write a recipe for making the sandwich.

Theme 5: Family Time

Reading Routines

Before You Read . . .

- Read the title of the story. Look closely at the picture on the cover. Guess what the story will be about.

While You Read . . .

- **Make predictions** about what you think Alex will do. Write your predictions in your journal. When you have finished the story, look back to see which of your predictions came true.

- **Use clues from the story to predict what will happen.** Read carefully, look at the pictures, and think about what you know of Alex. Use these clues to make your predictions.

Theme 5: Family Time

Punctuation Pizazz!

Using Exclamation Marks

Read aloud page 230 with a friend. Look at the sentences that end with exclamation marks (!). Why do you think the author uses these marks?

Take turns reading these sentences aloud again. Do you hear how your voice gets excited when you read these sentences? These sentences show strong feeling.

Write two or three sentences that end with exclamation marks. Read them to your friend.

Theme 5: Family Time

Literature Discussion

- Why is Alex unhappy on her birthday? Do you think she is right to be so upset?

- How does she show her feelings? What do you think of the way she acts?

- What has happened to the carousel that Alex's father gave her?

- Would you have tried to fix the carousel before falling asleep? Why or why not?

Theme 5: Family Time

How Do You Feel?

Mood

How does this story make you feel?

Draw a smiling face or a sad face to show how you feel. Then write this sentence under your drawing. Fill in the blanks.

This story makes me feel ___ because ___.

Share your drawing and your sentence with a friend.

Theme 5: Family Time

Reading Routines

Before You Read . . .

- Read the title of the story. Look closely at the picture on the cover. Guess what the story will be about.

While You Read . . .

- **Think of things that might happen next** in the story. Write them in your journal. As you read the story, see if things happen as you thought they would.

- **Reread sentences that are hard.** Look at the pictures again to help you understand the hard sentences.

Theme 5: Family Time

Is It Scientific?

Storm Tracking

Grandma has a way to figure out how far away a storm is. Is her way of doing this scientific?

Look in books and on the Internet to learn more about thunder and lightning.

Make notes about what you learn, and share them with the class.

Theme 5: Family Time

Literature Discussion

- What is the scariest thing about a thunder storm? Why do you think so?

- What is the scariest thing the girl has had to do so far?

- What does Grandma say, and how does she say it, to help the girl not be scared? Do you think it works?

Theme 5: Family Time

Thunder's Voice

Personification

Read aloud the last sentence on page 289. Does thunder really have a voice?

Sometimes writers describe things in nature as if they were human. How would you describe the wind as if it were human?

With a partner, write a sentence about wind, a tree, or a mountain. Describe it as if it were human.

Theme 5: Family Time

Reading Routines

Before You Read . . .

- Read the title and look at the the cover. Imagine some things that could happen during an art lesson.

While You Read . . .

- **Write in your journal** how you think Tommy feels.

- **Complete your What the Author Thinks Chart.** Look for clues that tell you what the author thinks about some art lessons in school. Use these clues to fill in the chart.

Theme 6: Talent Show

What's Fun?

Write a Story

Choose one of Tommy's friends described on page 354.

Write a story telling about the friend and the thing he or she likes to do most.

Be sure to use details that explain why this friend likes doing this activity.

Theme 6: Talent Show

Literature Discussion

- What do you think of how Tommy has handled his problem so far?

- What would you tell Tommy if you could talk to him?

- What in the stories and pictures tell you how Tom and Nana feel about Tommy's drawings?

- o you feel the way Tommy does about painting in k_____n? Why or why not?

Theme 6: Talent Show

The Name Game

Name Brainstorm

Work with a partner. Think of a name for Mrs. Bowers that would tell something about her job as an art teacher.

Brainstorm a list of art words, for example, chalk, brush, draw, red.

Make a word into a new name for the art teacher. For example, does Mrs. Bristle sound like an art teacher?

Theme 6: Talent Show

Reading Routines

Before You Read . . .

- Flip through the pages and look at the pictures to see what the story might be about.

While You Read . . .

- **Think of questions** you have about how people who are deaf could enjoy going to a concert.

- **Write in your journal** about your own experience at a concert or listening to an instrument.

Theme 6: Talent Show

Literature Discussion

- Have you ever felt the vibration of sound when listening to music or at other times? Tell about a time when you have felt sound vibrations.

- Have you ever broken your arm? How did you write? Have you ever sprained your ankle? How did you walk? Tell about a time when you had to find a different way to do something.

- If you could not hear, what are some sounds you would miss? What are some sounds you would not miss?

Theme 6: **Talent Show**

Be a Conductor!

Conducting Music

Listen to a recording of an orchestra. Pretend that you are the conductor of this orchestra. Your job is to lead the musicians as they play.

Have your friends pretend to play instruments, such as violins, drums, flutes, or a piano. As you listen to the music again, "conduct" your orchestra of friends. Use your face and arm movements to show the "musicians" when to begin and how fast to play.

Theme 6: Talent Show

What's My Sign?

Sign Language

Think about what job you would like to do when you grow up. Write a sentence describing that job.

Look in books and on the Internet to learn how to say the words in your sentence using sign language.

Then sign your sentence to your classmates to tell them what you want to be when you grow up. See if they can understand what you are saying.

Theme 6: Talent Show

Reading Routines

Before You Read . . .

- Read the title. Flip through the pages and look at the pictures to see what the story might be about.

While You Read . . .

- **Write in your journal** how you think the children feel about their school's celebration.

- **Complete your Solving Problems Chart.** Find examples from the story that tell how students solved the problems listed in the chart. Write the examples in the chart.

Theme 6: Talent Show

Cave Painting of Today

Mural Painting

Imagine that you want to create a mural so that people in the future will know what your life was like. Think of all the cool things you use that people didn't have even ten years ago!

- List things that you use or do every day. Tell why each is important to you.

- Then sketch pictures to show what the mural will look like.

Theme 6: Talent Show

Literature Discussion

- Why do you think Mrs. Sanchez had the class vote on which project they wanted to do? Do you think this was a fair or unfair way to make the decision? Why?

- What ideas could you give Mrs. Sanchez about the best way to choose a group project?

- Which project idea would you have voted for? Why?

- Besides a neighborhood and a school, what are some other scenes you could show in a mural?

Theme 6: Talent Show

Hey! That's My Neighborhood!

Mural Brainstorm

In a group, think of scenes you could paint on a mural to show people and places in your neighborhood.

Make a list of your mural ideas.

Theme 6: Talent Show

Observation Checklists

Theme 1

Record observations of student progress
for those areas important to you.

- = Beginning Understanding
√ = Developing Understanding
√+ = Proficient

Student Names

"Shopping" from Dragon Gets By							
Phonics: Short Vowels *a, i*							
Comprehension Strategy: Summarize							
Comprehension Skill: Story Structure							
Information & Study: Reading a Chart							
Spelling: The Short *a* and *i* Sounds							
Vocabulary Skill: Homophones							
High-Frequency Words							
Grammar: What Is a Sentence?							
Writing Skill: A Character Sketch							
Listening/Speaking/Viewing: Choral Retelling							

Reading-Writing Workshop:							
A Story							

Julius							
Phonics: Short Vowels *o, u, e;* Structural Analysis: VCCV Pattern							
Comprehension Strategy: Monitor/Clarify							
Comprehension Skill: Fantasy and Realism							
Information & Study: Using a Diagram							
Spelling: The Short *e, o,* and *u* Sounds							
Vocabulary Skill: Synonyms							
High-Frequency Words							
Grammar: Naming Parts of Sentences							
Writing Skill: Response-Journal Entry							
Listening/Speaking/Viewing: Group Discussion							

Record observations of student progress for those areas important to you.

− = Beginning Understanding
√ = Developing Understanding
√+ = Proficient

Student Names

Mrs. Brown Went to Town

Phonics: Long Vowels—CVCe: *a, i*						
Comprehension Strategy: Predict/Infer						
Comprehension Skill: Predicting Outcomes						
Information & Study: Locating Information						
Spelling: Vowel-Consonant-e Spellings						
Vocabulary Skill: Dictionary: Multiple-Meaning Words						
High-Frequency Words						
Grammar: Action Parts of Sentences						
Writing Skill: Journal Entry						
Listening/Speaking/Viewing: Have a Conversation						

General Observation

Independent Reading						
Independent Writing						
Work Habits						

Theme 2

Record observations of student progress for those areas important to you.

− = Beginning Understanding
√ = Developing Understanding
√+ = Proficient

Student Names

Henry and Mudge and the Starry Night

Phonics: Long Vowels—CVCe: *o, u, e;* Two Sounds for *g*						
Comprehension Strategy: Question						
Comprehension Skill: Compare and Contrast						
Information & Study: Using a Map						
Spelling: More Vowel-Consonant-e Spellings						
Vocabulary Skill: Compound Words						
High-Frequency Words						
Grammar: Telling Sentences and Questions						
Writing Skill: Writing an Answer to a Question						
Listening/Speaking/Viewing: Tell a Story						

Reading-Writing Workshop:

A Description						

Exploring Parks With Ranger Dockett

Phonics: Consonant Clusters; Two Sounds for *c*						
Comprehension Strategy: Evaluate						
Comprehension Skill: Fact and Opinion						
Information & Study: Using a Graph						
Spelling: Words with Consonant Clusters						
Vocabulary Skill: Antonyms						
High-Frequency Words						
Grammar: Commands						
Writing Skill: Writing a Paragraph						
Listening/Speaking/Viewing: Make a Presentation						

Observation Checklist

Record observations of student progress for those areas important to you.

- − = Beginning Understanding
- √ = Developing Understanding
- √+ = Proficient

Student Names

Around the Pond: Who's Been Here?						
Phonics: Double Consonants; **Structural Analysis: VCV Pattern**						
Comprehension Strategy: Monitor/Clarify						
Comprehension Skill: Categorize and Classify						
Information & Study: Using Guide Words in a Dictionary						
Spelling: Words with Double Consonants						
Vocabulary Skill: Multiple-Meaning Words						
High-Frequency Words						
Grammar: Exclamations						
Writing Skill: Writing a Learning-Log Entry						
Listening/Speaking/Viewing: **View Details in an Illustration**						

General Observation						
Independent Reading						
Independent Writing						
Work Habits						

Theme 3

Record observations of student progress for those areas important to you.

– = Beginning Understanding
√ = Developing Understanding
√+ = Proficient

	Student Names						
Chinatown							
Phonics: Consonant Digraphs *th, wh, sh, ch, (tch)*; Structural Analysis: Base Words and Endings *-er, -est*							
Comprehension Strategy: Summarize							
Comprehension Skill: Making Judgments							
Information & Study: Using a Schedule							
Spelling: Words Spelled with *th, wh, sh, ch (tch)*							
Vocabulary Skill: Dictionary: ABC Order to the Third Letter							
High-Frequency Words							
Grammar: Naming Words (Common Nouns)							
Writing Skill: Writing a Scene							
Listening/Speaking/Viewing: Tell a Story Through Drama							
Reading-Writing Workshop:							
A Friendly Letter							
A Trip to the Firehouse							
Phonics: Vowel Pairs *ai, ay*; Compound Words							
Comprehension Strategy: Question							
Comprehension Skill: Topic/Main Idea/Details							
Information & Study: Using the Phone Book							
Spelling: More Long *a* Spellings							
Vocabulary Skill: Beginning, Middle, and End							
High-Frequency Words							
Grammar: Special Nouns (Proper Nouns)							
Writing Skill: Taking Notes							
Listening/Speaking/Viewing: Give Personal Information							

Record observations of student progress
for those areas important to you.

− = Beginning Understanding
√ = Developing Understanding
√+ = Proficient

Student Names

Big Bushy Mustache							
Phonics: Vowel Pairs *ow, ou*; Structural Analysis: Suffixes *-ly, -ful*							
Comprehension Strategy: Predict/Infer							
Comprehension Skill: Problem Solving							
Information & Study: Understanding the Calendar							
Spelling: Vowel Sound in *cow*							
Vocabulary Skill: Using Context							
High-Frequency Words							
Grammar: One and More Than One							
Writing Skill: Problem-Solution Paragraph							
Listening/Speaking/Viewing: Make a Banner							
Jamaica Louise James							
Phonics: Vowel Pairs *ee, ea*; Structural Analysis: Common Syllables *-tion, -ture*							
Comprehension Strategy: Evaluate							
Comprehension Skill: Making Inferences							
Information & Study: Using an Encyclopedia							
Spelling: More Long *e* Spellings							
Vocabulary Skill: Using Guide Words in a Dictionary							
High-Frequency Words							
Grammar: Nouns That Change Spelling in Plural							
Writing Skill: Writing to Persuade							
Listening/Speaking/Viewing: View Illustrations of Characters							
General Observation							
Independent Reading							
Independent Writing							
Work Habits							

Theme 4

Record observations of student progress for those areas important to you.

- − = Beginning Understanding
- √ = Developing Understanding
- √+ = Proficient

Student Names

Officer Buckle and Gloria

Phonics: *r*-Controlled Vowels *ar, or, ore*						
Comprehension Strategy: Monitor/Clarify						
Comprehension Skill: Drawing Conclusions						
Information & Study: Interviewing						
Spelling: Vowel + *r* Sound in *car*						
Vocabulary Skill: Dictionary: Entry Words						
High-Frequency Words						
Grammar: Words for Nouns (Pronouns)						
Writing Skill: Writing an Invitation						
Listening/Speaking/Viewing: Give a Talk						

Reading-Writing Workshop:

A Research Report						

Ant

Phonics: Words with *nd, nt, mp, ng, nk;* Structural Analysis: Base Words and Endings -s, -es, -ies (nouns)						
Comprehension Strategy: Question						
Comprehension Skill: Text Organization						
Information & Study: Using a Glossary						
Spelling: Words That End with *nd, ng* or *nk*						
Vocabulary Skill: Using a Thesaurus						
High-Frequency Words						
Grammar: Singular Possessive Nouns						
Writing Skill: Writing a Poem						
Listening/Speaking/Viewing: Have a Group Discussion						

Student Names

Record observations of student progress
for those areas important to you.

− = Beginning Understanding
√ = Developing Understanding
√+ = Proficient

The Great Ball Game						
Phonics: Vowel Pairs *oa, ow*						
Comprehension Strategy: Summarize						
Comprehension Skill: Cause and Effect						
Information & Study: Following Directions						
Spelling: More Long *o* Spellings (*o, oa, ow*)						
Vocabulary Skill: Parts of a Dictionary Entry						
High-Frequency Words						
Grammar: Plural Possessive Nouns						
Writing Skill: Writing a News Article						
Listening/Speaking/Viewing: Give Clear Directions						

General Observation						
Independent Reading						
Independent Writing						
Work Habits						

Theme 5

Observation Checklist

Record observations of student progress for those areas important to you.

− = Beginning Understanding
√ = Developing Understanding
√+ = Proficient

Student Names

Brothers and Sisters

Phonics: The -er Ending in Two-Syllable Words						
Comprehension Strategy: Evaluate						
Comprehension Skill: Making Generalizations						
Information & Study: Timelines						
Spelling: Words That End with -er						
Vocabulary Skill: Word Families						
High-Frequency Words						
Grammar: Verbs						
Writing Skill: Writing an Opinion						
Listening/Speaking/Viewing: Make a Presentation						

Reading-Writing Workshop:

A Personal Narrative						

Jalapeño Bagels

Phonics: Structural Analysis: Contractions; The -le Ending in Two-Syllable Words						
Comprehension Strategy: Question						
Comprehension Skill: Following Directions						
Information & Study: Parts of a Book: Title Page and Table of Contents						
Spelling: Contractions						
Vocabulary Skill: Dictionary: Word Meanings						
High-Frequency Words						
Grammar: Verbs That Tell About Now						
Writing Skill: Responding to a Writing Prompt						
Listening/Speaking/Viewing: Describe a Photograph						

Student Names

Record observations of student progress for those areas important to you.

– = Beginning Understanding
√ = Developing Understanding
√+ = Proficient

Carousel						
Phonics: Sound of *y* at the End of Longer Words; The Prefix *un-*						
Comprehension Strategy: Predict/Infer						
Comprehension Skill: Making Judgments						
Information & Study: Reference Sources: Electronic Media						
Spelling: The Final Sound in *puppy*						
Vocabulary Skill: Homophones						
High-Frequency Words						
Grammar: Verbs That Tell About the Past						
Writing Skill: Writing an Information Paragraph						
Thunder Cake						
Phonics: Structural Analysis: Base Words and Endings *-ed*, *-ing* (Double Final Consonant); Silent Consonants *gh*, *k(n)*, *b*						
Comprehension Strategy: Monitor/Clarify						
Comprehension Skill: Sequence of Events						
Information & Study: Taking Notes						
Spelling: Words That End with *-ed or -ing*						
Vocabulary Skill: Dictionary: Finding Words with Endings						
High-Frequency Words						
Grammar: The Verb *is/are, was/were*						
Writing Skill: Dialogue						
Listening/Speaking/Viewing: Put On a Play						
General Observation						
Independent Reading						
Independent Writing						
Work Habits						

Theme 6

Record observations of student progress
for those areas important to you.

− = Beginning Understanding
√ = Developing Understanding
√+ = Proficient

Student Names

The Art Lesson

Phonics: Vowel Pairs *oo, ew, ue, ou*						
Comprehension Strategy: Evaluate						
Comprehension Skill: Author's Viewpoint						
Information & Study: Using a Newspaper						
Spelling: Vowel Sounds in *moon* and *book*						
Vocabulary Skill: Word Families						
High-Frequency Words						
Grammar: Other Irregular Verbs						
Writing Skill: Paragraph That Explains						
Listening/Speaking/Viewing: Compare/Contrast Illustrations						

Reading-Writing Workshop:

Instructions						

Moses Goes to a Concert

Phonics: Long *i* (*igh, ie*)						
Comprehension Strategy: Summarize						
Comprehension Skill: Noting Details						
Information & Study: Captions						
Spelling: More Long *i* Spellings (*y, i, igh*)						
Vocabulary Skill: More Multiple-Meaning Words						
High-Frequency Words						
Grammar: Adjectives Including *a, an,* and *the*						
Writing Skill: Summary						
Listening/Speaking/Viewing: Nonverbal Cues						

Student Names

Record observations of student progress for those areas important to you.

− = Beginning Understanding
√ = Developing Understanding
√+ = Proficient

The School Mural						
Phonics: Structural Analysis: Base Words Endings -ed, -ing (drop final e)						
Comprehension Strategy: Question						
Comprehension Skill: Problem Solving						
Information & Study: Chapter Titles and Headings						
Spelling: More Words with -ed or -ing						
Vocabulary Skill: Using Context						
High-Frequency Words						
Grammar: Comparing with Adjectives						
Writing Skill: News Article						
Listening/Speaking/Viewing: Persuasive Talk						

General Observation						
Independent Reading						
Independent Writing						
Work Habits						

Observation Checklists

Selection Tests and Answer Keys

Dragon Gets By

Write your answers to these questions. Look back at the selection for help.

1. Strategy Focus: Summarizing Tell in your own words what happens after Dragon eats all the food.

_____

_____

_____

2. How is the beginning of the story like the end of the story?

_____

_____

_____

Choose the best answer and fill in the circle.

3. Which of the following is NOT a place where action happens in the story?

○ **a.** the store

○ **b.** Dragon's house

○ **c.** Dragon's school

○ **d.** the parking lot

Test Continues ➡

Dragon Gets By (continued)

4. Why didn't Dragon have any food when he got home from the store?

○ **a.** He ate all the food he bought before he went home.

○ **b.** He didn't buy any food at the store.

○ **c.** All the food rolled out of the car on the way home.

○ **d.** He gave the food to friends.

Read the sentence and choose the best answer.

5. Dragon was not a very good <u>shopper</u>.

What is the meaning of <u>shopper</u> in this sentence?

○ **a.** a person who acts silly

○ **b.** a person who makes messes

○ **c.** a person who drives a car

○ **d.** a person who buys things

6. Dragon should eat a <u>balanced</u> meal.

What kind of meal should he have?

○ **a.** food that is not good for you

○ **b.** not too much of any one thing

○ **c.** too much of everything

○ **d.** food that is hot

Julius

Write your answers to these questions. Look back at the selection for help.

1. **Strategy Focus: Monitor/Clarify** What can you ask yourself to monitor your reading? What can you do if something doesn't make sense?

_____

_____

_____

_____

2. Why do you think the author used fantasy details in this story?

_____

_____

_____

_____

Choose the best answer and fill in the circle.

3. Which of the following COULD really happen?

○ **a.** A pig sneaks into a store to try on clothes.

○ **b.** A pig hugs a little girl.

○ **c.** A pig stays up late to watch movies on TV.

○ **d.** A pig makes noise.

Test Continues →

Julius (continued)

4. Maya's Granddaddy gave her Julius to teach her fun and sharing. Maya had always wanted a horse or an older brother. What do these things tell you?

- ○ **a.** Maya wants Granddaddy to visit more.
- ○ **b.** Maya needs to spend more time at school.
- ○ **c.** Maya was lonely before Julius came.
- ○ **d.** Maya wants to take Julius to show and tell.

Read the sentence and choose the best answer.

5. Did you hear a soft <u>sound</u>?

Which word means the same as <u>sound</u>?

- ○ **a.** voice
- ○ **b.** band
- ○ **c.** noise
- ○ **d.** clap

6. *He <u>slurped</u> coffee and ate too much peanut butter.*

What is the meaning of <u>slurped</u>?

- ○ **a.** drank in a noisy way
- ○ **b.** spilled all over
- ○ **c.** sniffed to see if it smelled good
- ○ **d.** mixed and stirred

Mrs. Brown Went to Town

Write your answers to these questions. Look back at the selection for help.

1. **Strategy Focus: Predict/Infer** From the text on the first page of the story, what can you figure out about what will happen?

   _____

   _____

   _____

2. What do you think Mrs. Brown would have done if the barn had fallen apart instead of her house?

   _____

   _____

   _____

Choose the best answer and fill in the circle.

3. The mouse voted not to move into Mrs. Brown's house and didn't do it. What would the mouse probably do if the other animals voted to move to the city and he voted not to?

   ○ **a.** move to the city anyway

   ○ **b.** visit them at the hospital

   ○ **c.** stay on the farm

   ○ **d.** ask Mrs. Brown for help

   Test Continues ➡

Mrs. Brown Went to Town (continued)

4. Why did Mrs. Brown have to go to the hospital the first time?

- ○ **a.** She had to be X-rayed and tested.
- ○ **b.** She had to drop off a letter.
- ○ **c.** She needed to rest.
- ○ **d.** She was bitten by a dog.

Read the sentence and choose the best answer.

5. *All this* <u>commotion</u> *woke Mrs. Brown*
In time to feel her bed crashing down!

In the sentence above, what does <u>commotion</u> mean?

- ○ **a.** a copy of something else
- ○ **b.** noisy excitement
- ○ **c.** talking and telling secrets
- ○ **d.** sounds animals make

6. Who <u>delivered</u> the letter to her friends?

What is the meaning of <u>delivered</u>?

- ○ **a.** handed over
- ○ **b.** wrote
- ○ **c.** won in a contest
- ○ **d.** set free

Name: _____

Henry and Mudge and the Starry Night

Write your answers to these questions. Look back at the selection for help.

1. Strategy Focus: Question What are two questions you can ask about the second page of the story?

_____

_____

_____

2. How was what Henry did on the good smelly hike different from what Mudge did on the good smelly hike?

_____

_____

_____

Choose the best answer and fill in the circle.

3. How was Mudge's backpack different from Henry's and his parents'?

○ **a.** Mudge's backpack was empty.

○ **b.** Mudge's backpack had the tent.

○ **c.** Mudge's backpack had lots of crackers.

○ **d.** Mudge's backpack had the pans and lanterns.

Test Continues ➡

Henry and Mudge and the Starry Night (continued)

4. Which of the following tells about Big Bear Lake?

○ **a.** Big Bear Lake is a city park with places to climb and slide.

○ **b.** Big Bear Lake is a flat, sandy place by the sea.

○ **c.** Big Bear Lake is a green place with trees, waterfalls, and streams.

○ **d.** Big Bear Lake is a street with shops and fast food places.

Read the sentence and choose the best answer.

5. *They parked the car and got ready to <u>hike</u>.*
What did they get ready to do?

○ **a.** pack things up

○ **b.** look for something that was lost

○ **c.** make the car move

○ **d.** take a long walk

6. Dad hung the <u>lantern</u> by the tent so we could see.
What is a <u>lantern</u>?

○ **a.** a container for holding a light

○ **b.** a kind of cooking pot

○ **c.** something worn on the back

○ **d.** something that can be plugged in

Name: _____

Exploring Parks with Ranger Dockett

Write your answers to these questions. Look back at the selection for help.

1. **Strategy Focus: Evaluate** Do you like the part of the story that tells how Ranger Dockett became a ranger? Why or why not?

_____

_____

_____

2. Is the following sentence a fact or an opinion? How do you know?
Ranger Dockett has the best job in the city.

_____

_____

_____

Choose the best answer and fill in the circle.

3. Which of the following is a FACT from the story?

○ **a.** Ranger Dockett's classes are the best.

○ **b.** Ranger Dockett is nicer than other rangers.

○ **c.** Ranger Dockett plants trees each year.

○ **d.** Ranger Dockett should not get in mud.

Test Continues ➡

Exploring Parks with Ranger Dockett (continued)

4. Which important idea below does the following sentence belong with?

   His students look for turtles, frogs, and insects.

   ○ **a.** Ranger Dockett teaches classes at the pond.

   ○ **b.** Ranger Dockett lives in New York City.

   ○ **c.** Ranger Dockett keeps in touch with other rangers.

   ○ **d.** Ranger Dockett makes people follow park rules.

Read the sentence and choose the best answer.

5. *He shows them how to <u>protect</u> the plants and animals that live there.*

   In the sentence above, what does <u>protect</u> mean?

   ○ **a.** to make grow

   ○ **b.** to study

   ○ **c.** to set free

   ○ **d.** to keep from harm

6. Parks are important in big, busy <u>urban</u> places. Which place below is an <u>urban</u> place?

   ○ **a.** a farm

   ○ **b.** a city

   ○ **c.** a forest

   ○ **d.** a lake

Around the Pond: Who's Been Here?

Write your answers to these questions. Look back at the selection for help.

1. **Strategy Focus: Monitor/Clarify** What can readers do when they don't understand something in a story?

   _____

   _____

2. Choose at least three words that are alike in some way. Write them in a list. Write a title for your list.

   path   tree   warm   muggy

   sunny   plants   pond   moss

   _____

   _____

   _____

Choose the best answer and fill in the circle.

3. Cammy and William see feathers, shells, and scales.

   Which group describes the things they see?

   ○ **a.** ways animals move

   ○ **b.** foods animals eat

   ○ **c.** animal body coverings

   ○ **d.** places animals live

Test Continues ➡

Around the Pond: Who's Been Here? (continued)

4. In the story, you learn that Sam likes blueberries. From this, what can you tell has happened?

○ **a.** Cammy and her brother threw a stick to Sam.

○ **b.** Cammy and her brother looked for Sam.

○ **c.** Cammy and her brother went for a swim.

○ **d.** Cammy and her brother fed Sam blueberries.

Read the sentence and choose the best answer.

5. *A dead sugar maple stands alone by the water's* <u>edge</u>.

In the sentence above, what does edge mean?

○

○ . a line or place where something ends

c. a track made by footsteps

○ **d.** the most important part of something

6. The pond was <u>shallow</u> in parts and deep in other parts.

What is the meaning of <u>shallow</u>?

○ **a.** not deep

○ **b.** dark

○ **c.** cold

○ **d.** not clean

Chinatown

Write your answers to these questions. Look back at the selection for help.

1. **Strategy Focus: Summarize** Sum up the part of the story that tells about Chinatown waking up. How does summing up help you as you read?

_____

_____

_____

2. In the story, Grandma tells the boy to stay close by at the Chinese New Year celebration. Is this a good idea? Explain your answer.

_____

_____

_____

Choose the best answer and fill in the circle.

3. Which names the group for these things in the story?

parade, lion dance, firecrackers

○ **a.** stores in Chinatown

○ **b.** classes in Chinatown

○ **c.** what Grandma and the boy see every day in Chinatown

○ **d.** parts of Chinese New Year celebration

Test Continues ➡

Chinatown (continued)

4. Which of the following is NOT true about the little boy in the story?

- ○ **a.** He cares about his grandmother.
- ○ **b.** He takes kung fu lessons.
- ○ **c.** He lives in the country.
- ○ **d.** His favorite holiday is Chinese New Year.

Read the sentence and choose the best answer.

5. *During the celebrations, the streets of Chinatown are always crowded.*

What are celebrations?

- ○ **a.** activities on a special day
- ○ **b.** things people do to make money
- ○ **c.** long walks
- ○ **d.** quick trips through a place

6. In Chinatown, the market is filled with shoppers.

What is the meaning of market?

- ○ **a.** a room or group of rooms to live in
- ○ **b.** a place where food and other things are sold
- ○ **c.** the place where an animal lives
- ○ **d.** a place to check out books

A Trip to the Firehouse

Write your answers to these questions. Look back at the selection for help.

1. Strategy Focus: Question What questions can you ask as you read the part of the story that is about the pole in the firehouse?

_____

_____

_____

_____

2. What point does the author want to make when she tells about the pole?

_____

_____

_____

_____

Choose the best answer and fill in the circle.

3. What would be a good heading for the part of the story about the different kinds of fire trucks?

○ **a.** Fire Trucks for Different Jobs

○ **b.** Rooms in the Firehouse

○ **c.** Meet the Firefighters

○ **d.** Spot, the Firehouse Dog

Test Continues ➡

A Trip to the Firehouse (continued)

4. At the beginning of the story, the children feed Spot. Which of these happens BEFORE the children feed Spot?

○ **a.** The children wave to the firefighters as they leave for a fire.

○ **b.** The fire chief greets the children.

○ **c.** The children have a snack.

○ **d.** The children help wash the fire truck.

Read the sentence and choose the best answer.

5. The firefighters put on their <u>gear</u> and jumped onto the truck.

In the sentence above, what does <u>gear</u> mean?

○ **a.** part of a machine that moves

○ **b.** to get ready to do something

○ **c.** special equipment used to do things

○ **d.** a kind of truck that firefighters drive

6. The children thanked the firehouse <u>leader</u>.

Who is the <u>leader</u> at the firehouse?

○ **a.** the teacher

○ **b.** the student

○ **c.** the father

○ **d.** the chief

Selection Tests

Big Bushy Mustache

Write your answers to these questions. Look back at the selection for help.

1. Strategy Focus: Predict/Infer Why did Ricky want to wear the mustache?

_____

_____

_____

2. When Ricky lost the mustache, he tried to solve his problem. He made a paper mustache. He put shoe polish above his lip. He made a mustache of shoe strings. If Ricky had to use one of those ideas, which one would be best? Why?

_____

_____

_____

Choose the best answer and fill in the circle.

3. In the story, Ricky has several problems. Which is the hardest problem to solve?

○ **a.** He wants to look like his father.

○ **b.** He can't decide what to be in the play.

○ **c.** He loses the mustache.

○ **d.** He can't tell Papi about the mustache.

Test Continues ➡

Big Bushy Mustache (continued)

4. Which of the following is NOT a place where things happen in the story?

   ○ **a.** Ricky's house

   ○ **b.** at the store

   ○ **c.** Ricky's school

   ○ **d.** on the street

Read the sentence and choose the best answer.

5. *It wasn't just a bushy* disguise *anymore, but a gift from his papi.*

   What is a disguise ?

   ○ **a.** something people wear to hide what they really look like

   ○ **b.** a piece of glass you can see yourself in

   ○ **c.** a kind of toy children play with

   ○ **d.** a part of Cinco de Mayo celebrations

6. Ricky had fun wearing the bushy mustache.

   Which word means almost the same as bushy ?

   ○ **a.** part of a plant

   ○ **b.** something that itches and tickles

   ○ **c.** large

   ○ **d.** fluffy

Jamaica Louise James

**Write your answers to these questions. Look back at the
selection for help.**

1. Strategy Focus: Evaluate What do you think about
the part of the story where everyone shouts,
"Surprise"? If it is your favorite part of the story, tell
why. If it is not your favorite part, tell which part is,
and why you like it best.

_____

_____

_____

2. How did the mayor feel about Jamaica's cool idea?
How do you know?

_____

_____

_____

Choose the best answer and fill in the circle.

3. In the story, Jamaica says, _But I paint, blending all
those colors until they look just right._

What does this tell you about Jamaica?

○ **a.** She likes to tell stories.

○ **b.** She works hard on her art.

○ **c.** She wants to visit new places.

○ **d.** She is learning to sew.

Test Continues ➡

Jamaica Louise James (continued)

4. Which event happens BEFORE Jamaica's 8th birthday?

○ **a.** Jamaica gets her cool idea.

○ **b.** People talk about the paintings in the subway station.

○ **c.** Jamaica and her mom go to the subway station on Grammy's birthday.

○ **d.** Jamaica draws from the top step of her building.

Read the sentence and choose the best answer.

5. *They give her a dollar or four quarters, and she slides a <u>token</u> into their hand.*

What is a <u>token</u>?

○ **a.** a piece of metal, like a coin, used to get into a certain place

○ **b.** a piece of artwork

○ **c.** something to read, like a newspaper

○ **d.** a light used to see in the dark

6. Grammy sells something at a <u>booth</u> in the subway.

What is a <u>booth</u>?

○ **a.** part of the train

○ **b.** a bank

○ **b.** a small room

○ **d.** a fast food place

Selection Tests

Officer Buckle and Gloria

Write your answers to these questions. Look back at the selection for help.

1. **Strategy Focus: Monitor/Clarify** What can you do if you are not sure about what is happening in part of the story?

   _____

   _____

   _____

2. How did the illustrations help you figure out why the children began listening to Officer Buckle when Gloria was with him?

   _____

   _____

   _____

Choose the best answer and fill in the circle.

3. Why didn't Officer Buckle know what Gloria was doing at first?

   ○ **a.** When he checked on her, she would sit at attention.

   ○ **b.** Officer Buckle was asleep.

   ○ **c.** Officer Buckle was still at the police station.

   ○ **d.** When he asked the children, they said nothing was happening.

Test Continues ➡

Officer Buckle and Gloria (continued)

4. Why did so many people ask Officer Buckle and Gloria to speak at their schools?

○ **a.** They had been having a lot of accidents.

○ **b.** They were studying a safety unit.

○ **c.** They wanted to see Gloria's tricks.

○ **d.** They wanted to eat ice cream after the speech.

Read the sentence and choose the best answer.

5. *"Gloria obeys my commands. Gloria, SIT!"*
   In the sentence above, what are commands?

○ **a.** jokes

○ **b.** questions

○ **c.** orders

○ **d.** plans

6. Would you like to be in the audience for Officer Buckle's speech?

What is an audience?

○ **a.** a group that listens and watches

○ **b.** a group of players at a sports event

○ **c.** a school

○ **d.** a television show

Ant

Write your answers to these questions. Look back at the selection for help.

1. Strategy Focus: Question The story tells about ant colonies and anthills. What are two questions you could ask a classmate about this part of the story?

_____

_____

2. In the story, one picture has the caption, *ants carrying dead stick insect, Brazil.* How does the caption, or words under the picture, help you as you read?

_____

_____

Choose the best answer and fill in the circle.

3. In the part of the story about army ants, how does the author show the important idea?

○ **a.** The author tells how all ants are the same.

○ **b.** The author tells the important idea and then supports it with details.

○ **c.** The author tells what happens in order.

○ **d.** The author tells a problem and a solution.

Test Continues ➡

Ant (continued)

4. Which of the following is an OPINION from the story?

○ **a.** Every ant has two long stalks on its head.

○ **b.** Carpenter ants live in wood.

○ **c.** I think ants are a lot like us.

○ **d.** Some ants eat juices that come from other insects.

Read the sentence and choose the best answer.

5. *A yellow fungus grows on the paste, and the ants eat the fungus.*

What is a fungus?

○ **a.** a very young ant or other insect

○ **b.** a group of insects that live together

○ **c.** a part of a plant that grows underground

○ **d.** a kind of plant without leaves or flowers

6. The ants work hard to build their tunnels.

What are tunnels?

○ **a.** long holes under the ground

○ **b.** piles of dirt on a sidewalk

○ **c.** a shortcut between tree branches

○ **d.** piles of yellow sawdust on a log

Name:_____

The Great Ball Game

Write your answers to these questions. Look back at the selection for help.

1. **Strategy Focus: Summarize** Sum up the beginning of the story where Crane and Bear have their idea. How does summarizing help you when you read?

_____

_____

_____

2. The story explains why birds fly south each winter. According to the story, why do birds fly south?

_____

_____

_____

Choose the best answer and fill in the circle.

3. In the game, Bat does not need light to find his way. What happens because Bat does not need light?

○ **a.** The Birds ask Bat to join their team.

○ **b.** Bat stumbles and falls.

○ **c.** Bear asks Bat to let the other animals play first.

○ **d.** Bat makes his way across the field with the ball.

Test Continues ➡

The Great Ball Game (continued)

4. How are Crane, the leader of the Birds, and Bear, the leader of the Animals, alike?

○ **a.** They are both kind to Bat.

○ **b.** They are both angry because they will have to leave for the winter.

○ **c.** They both have the idea of a ball game to settle the argument.

○ **d.** They both see good things about the other group.

Read the sentence and choose the best answer.

5. *The side that loses will have to* <u>accept</u> *the penalty given by the other side.*

In the sentence above, what does <u>accept</u> mean?

○ **a.** talk about

○ **b.** take care of

○ **c.** agree to

○ **d.** make it look easy

6. The Birds and Animals must settle their <u>quarrel</u>.

What is a <u>quarrel</u>?

○ **a.** a game

○ **b.** an argument

○ **c.** a kind of punishment

○ **d.** an answer

Brothers and Sisters

Write your answers to these questions. Look back at the selection for help.

1. **Strategy Focus: Evaluate** Do you like the part of the story where Peter talks about being a younger brother? Why or why not?

   _____

   _____

   _____

2. From reading about twins in the story, what can you say is true about most twins?

   _____

   _____

   _____

Choose the best answer and fill in the circle.

3. From reading the story, what can you say is true about brothers and sisters?

   ○ **a.** All are mad because their moms spend time with babies.

   ○ **b.** Most brothers and sisters never fight.

   ○ **c.** Most get along sometimes and have problems sometimes.

   ○ **d.** All are always good helpers with babies.

   Test Continues ➡

4. What would be another good title for this story?

   ○ **a.** Children in Families

   ○ **b.** When a New Baby Comes

   ○ **c.** How It Feels to Be the Youngest

   ○ **d.** Always Best Friends

5. *Ben has a newborn brother, and Darrie has a new sister.*

   In the sentence above, what does <u>newborn</u> mean?

   ○ **a.** two children born at the same time to the same parents

   ○ **b.** older than the first child

   ○ **c.** having a different mom and dad

   ○ **d.** only a few days or weeks old

6. I will *distract* the baby so she won't cry.

   What is the meaning of <u>distract</u>?

   ○ **a.** to say the baby is cute

   ○ **b.** to put the baby to sleep

   ○ **c.** to get the baby to think about something else

   ○ **d.** to be friends with the baby

Jalapeño Bagels

Write your answers to these questions. Look back at the selection for help.

1. **Strategy Focus: Question** Write two questions to ask about the part of the story where Mamá tells Pablo he can take a treat from the *panadería* to school.

_____

_____

_____

2. The story has two recipes at the end. Write at least two things you should do when you follow any directions, such as a recipe.

_____

_____

_____

Choose the best answer and fill in the circle.

3. In the story, Pablo and Papá let the bagels rise, boil them, then bake them. What would happen if one day they baked them first and then boiled them?

   ○ **a.** The bagels would not turn out well.

   ○ **b.** There would be no cream cheese.

   ○ **c.** They would forget to put on the poppy seeds.

   ○ **d.** The bagels would not rise.

Test Continues ➡

Jalapeño Bagels (continued)

4. How are jalapeño bagels different from the other bakery treats?

   ○ **a.** They have flour in them.

   ○ **b.** They are baked in the oven.

   ○ **c.** They are a mix of two cultures.

   ○ **d.** They are made by Pablo's mother and father.

   dulce.

   What does <u>ingredients</u> mean?

   ○ **a.** hot green peppers

   ○ **b.** tools for cooking

   ○ **c.** parts of a mixture

   ○ **d.** steps to follow

6. Many <u>buyers</u> come to the bakery on Saturday.

   Which word means the same as <u>buyers</u>?

   ○ **a.** customers

   ○ **b.** rangers

   ○ **c.** workers

   ○ **d.** audience

Carousel

Write your answers to these questions. Look back at the selection for help.

1. **Strategy Focus: Predict/Infer** Alex didn't want cake after dinner with just her aunts. From this clue, what can you predict about the story?

    _____

    _____

    _____

2. Was it fair that Alex's mom sent her to bed without any birthday cake? Why or why not?

    _____

    _____

    _____

Choose the best answer and fill in the circle.

3. What do you think Alex's mother would do if Alex was mean to a friend who came to play?

    ○ **a.** She would not do anything.

    ○ **b.** She would make Alex go to her room for a while.

    ○ **c.** She would give Alex and her friend a treat.

    ○ **d.** She would ask Alex's dad to do something with Alex.

Test Continues →

Carousel (continued)

4. What was the real reason Alex wasn't nice about the presents from her aunts?

○ **a.** She was unhappy because she wanted cake first.

○ **b.** She was sad because she wanted them to give her a bat and ball.

○ **c.** She was mad at her aunts because they were making a fuss.

○ **d.** She was upset because her dad wasn't there.

Read the sentence and choose the best answer.

5. "No way," Alex groaned.

What kind of sound did Alex make when she groaned?

○ **a.** a deep moaning sound

○ **b.** a funny sound

○ **c.** a long yell

○ **d.** a soft, quiet sound

6. Alex was angry because her dad couldn't be there.

How did Alex feel?

○ **a.** bored

○ **b.** glad

○ **c.** mad

○ **d.** afraid

Name: _____

Thunder Cake

Write your answers to these questions. Look back at the selection for help.

1. **Strategy Focus: Monitor/Clarify** What can you ask yourself to make sure you understand every part of the story? What can you do if you do not understand something?

_____

_____

_____

_____

2. Why is it important to Grandma to get the cake into the oven before the storm comes?

_____

_____

_____

Choose the best answer and fill in the circle.

3. Which of these happens AFTER Grandma and the girl put the Thunder Cake into the oven?

   ○ **a.** The thunder and lightning begin.

   ○ **b.** The girl hides under the bed.

   ○ **c.** The girl gathers eggs.

   ○ **d.** The girl says she is brave.

Test Continues →

Thunder Cake (continued)

4. What lesson did Grandma want to teach?

○ **a.** A cake needs butter and strawberries.

○ **b.** A storm is about ten miles away.

○ **c.** Thunder is only a loud noise.

○ **d.** It's best to hide from thunder and lightning.

Read the sentence and choose the best answer.

5. *We were by the barn door when a huge <u>bolt</u> of lightning flashed.*

In the sentence above, what does <u>bolt</u> mean?

○ **a.** a sound

○ **b.** a flash or stroke

○ **c.** a thick block

○ **d.** a loud noise

6. We saw the sun peek over the <u>horizon</u>.

What does <u>horizon</u> mean?

○ **a.** the very top of a hill

○ **b.** body of water, like a lake

○ **c.** the line where earth and sky seem to meet

○ **d.** a deep dip in the land

The Art Lesson

Write your answers to these questions. Look back at the selection for help.

1. **Strategy Focus: Evaluate** What do you like about the part of the story where Tommy tells Mrs. Bowers he is going to be an artist when he grows up? What do you dislike? Give reasons for your answers.

_____

_____

_____

_____

2. What do you think the author of *The Art Lesson* thinks about making art?

_____

_____

_____

Choose the best answer and fill in the circle.

3. Why did the author write *The Art Lesson*?

   ○ **a.** to explain how to draw a Pilgrim man

   ○ **b.** to describe what happened to him as a boy

   ○ **c.** to ask people to draw more

   ○ **d.** to tell his feelings about his grandparents

Test Continues ➡

The Art Lesson (continued)

4. What clues in the story tell you that the author's family is important to him?

   ○ **a.** The author writes about his mom, dad, brother, cousins, and grandparents.

   ○ **b.** The author writes about drawing on the walls.

   ○ **c.** The author writes about his birthday present.

   ○ **d.** The author writes about drawing on his sheets.

Read the sentence and choose the best answer.

5. *"And remember, don't <u>ruin</u> it, because it is the only piece you'll get."*

   In the sentence above, what does <u>ruin</u> mean?

   ○ **a.** to make bigger

   ○ **b.** to clean up

   ○ **c.** to lose something

   ○ **d.** to hurt or spoil

6. I always put on a <u>smock</u> before I paint.

   What is a <u>smock</u>?

   ○ **a.** a kind of shirt worn over clothes to protect them

   ○ **b.** a kind of covering for shoes

   ○ **c.** a kind of smile, like a grin

   ○ **d.** a kind of thick coat to keep from getting cold

Moses Goes to a Concert

Write your answers to these questions. Look back at the selection for help.

1. **Strategy Focus: Summarize** Sum up what you learn about Moses in the beginning of the story.

   _____

   _____

   _____

   _____

2. What does Moses notice about how the percussionist is dressed? How is that important to the story?

   _____

   _____

   _____

Choose the best answer and fill in the circle.

3. What are two ways Moses feels music in the story?
   - ○ **a.** by holding hands; by signing
   - ○ **b.** by holding a balloon; through stocking feet
   - ○ **c.** by riding a bus; by clapping
   - ○ **d.** by waving to friends; by walking on stage

Test Continues ➡

Moses Goes to a Concert (continued)

4. Which of these is true about percussionists?

○ **a.** They play instruments you blow into, such as flutes.

○ **b.** They play all kinds of instruments.

○ **c.** They play instruments you hit, such as drums.

○ **d.** They play instruments with strings, such as guitars.

Read the sentence and choose the best answer.

5. *She follows the orchestra by feeling the* <u>*vibrations*</u> *of the music through her stocking feet.*

In the sentence above, what does <u>vibrations</u> mean?

○ **a.** a quick moving back and forth

○ **b.** a flash or stroke

○ **c.** a deep, rolling sound

○ **d.** a set of directions for making something

6. Ms. Elwyn became <u>deaf</u> after she was very ill.

What was Ms. Elwyn NOT able to do?

○ **a.** walk

○ **b.** see

○ **c.** eat

○ **d.** hear

The School Mural

Write your answers to these questions. Look back at the selection for help.

1. **Strategy Focus: Question** Write two good questions you can ask about murals after you understand what a mural is.

   _____

   _____

   _____

2. In the story, Paul slips and puts his handprints on the mural. The other children decide to add their handprints, too. How would you have solved the problem of having handprints on the mural?

   _____

   _____

   _____

Choose the best answer and fill in the circle.

3. Why did the children think the mural was the best idea?
   - ○ **a.** They could make it on a computer.
   - ○ **b.** A mural was on the wall of the pet shop.
   - ○ **c.** Everyone could help make a mural.
   - ○ **d.** Murals were painted long ago in caves.

Test Continues ➡

The School Mural (continued)

4. Which of these happened BEFORE the children chose the mural project?

   ○ **a.** They talked about their project ideas.

   ○ **b.** They asked the principal if they could paint a mural.

   ○ **c.** A reporter came to write a story.

   ○ **d.** They asked the art teacher to help.

Read the sentence and choose the best answer.

5. *First, they planned the <u>scenes</u> to draw.*

   In the sentence above, what does <u>scenes</u> mean?

   ○ **a.** pictures or views

   ○ **b.** parts of a group

   ○ **c.** what people wear

   ○ **d.** things artists use to make artwork

6. *The headline said, "Children Show School <u>Pride</u>."*

   What kind of feeling is <u>pride</u>?

   ○ **a.** the feeling of being afraid of something

   ○ **b.** the feeling of being mad about something

   ○ **c.** the feeling of being proud of something

   ○ **d.** the feeling of being sad about something

ANSWER KEY

THEME 1

Selection 1

Dragon Gets By

Sample answers provided for questions 1 and 2.

1. Dragon won't fit into his car, so he rolls the car home. Then he is hungry. But he ate all the food he bought, so he has to go shopping again. *(Reading Strategy: Summarize)* (1 Point)
2. Dragon has the same problem. He is hungry, and he doesn't have any food in the house. *(story structure)* (1)
3. **c.** Dragon's school *(story structure)* (1)
4. **a.** He ate all the food he bought before he went home. *(cause and effect)* (1)
5. **d.** a person who buys things *(key vocabulary)* (1)
6. **b.** not too much of any one thing *(key vocabulary)* (1)

Assessment Tip: Total 6 Points

Selection 2

Julius

Sample answers provided for questions 1 and 2.

1. Did I understand what I read? Are there things that don't make sense? I can go back and reread to see if that will help things make sense. *(Reading Strategy: Monitor/Clarify)* (1 Point)
2. The fantasy makes the story funny. A make-believe pig can do more funny things than a real pig. *(fantasy/realism)* (1)
3. **d.** A pig makes noise. *(fantasy/realism)* (1)
4. **c.** Maya was lonely before Julius came. *(drawing conclusions)* (1)
5. **c.** noise *(key vocabulary)* (1)
6. **a.** drank in a noisy way *(key vocabulary)* (1)

Assessment Tip: Total 6 Points

Selection 3

Mrs. Brown Went to Town

Sample answers provided for questions 1 and 2.

1. Something is going to happen that will make Mrs. Brown live in the barn. *(Reading Strategy: Predict/Infer)* (1 Point)
2. She would have moved the animals into her house. *(predicting outcomes)* (1)
3. **c.** stay on the farm *(predicting outcomes)* (1)
4. **d.** She was bitten by a dog. *(cause and effect)* (1)
5. **b.** noisy excitement *(key vocabulary)* (1)
6. **a.** handed over *(key vocabulary)* (1)

Assessment Tip: Total 6 Points

ANSWER KEY

THEME 2

Selection 1

Henry and Mudge and the Starry Night

Sample answers provided for questions 1 and 2.

1. How does Henry's mother know about camping? What does she know how to do? *(Reading Strategy: Question)* (1 Point)
2. Henry looked at everything. Mudge didn't see anything. He just smelled along the trail. *(compare and contrast)* (1)
3. **c.** Mudge's backpack had lots of crackers. *(compare and contrast)* (1)
4. **c.** Big Bear Lake is a green place with trees, waterfalls, and streams. *(story structure)* (1)
5. **d.** take a long walk *(key vocabulary)* (1)
6. **a.** a container for holding a light *(key vocabulary)* (1)

Assessment Tip: Total 6 Points

Selection 2

Exploring Parks with Ranger Dockett

Sample answers provided for questions 1 and 2.

1. Answers will vary. *(Reading Strategy: Evaluate)* (1 Point)
2. The sentence is an opinion. It tells what someone thinks. You cannot show that it is true or false. *(fact and opinion)* (1)
3. **c.** Ranger Dockett plants trees each year. *(fact and opinion)* (1)
4. **a.** Ranger Dockett teaches classes at the pond. *(topic/main idea/details)* (1)
5. **d.** to keep from harm *(key vocabulary)* (1)
6. **b.** a city *(key vocabulary)* (1)

Assessment Tip: Total 6 Points

Selection 3

Around the Pond: Who's Been Here?

Sample answers provided for questions 1 and 2.

1. When readers don't understand something in a story, they can reread to try to figure things out. *(Reading Strategy: Monitor/Clarify)* (1 Point)
2. Answers will vary, but words should be related and the title of the list should explain the relatedness. *(categorize and classify)* (1)
3. **c.** animal body coverings *(categorize and classify)* (1)
4. **d.** Cammy and her brother fed Sam blueberries, or he took some and ate them. *(drawing conclusions)* (1)
5. **b.** a line or place where something ends *(key vocabulary)* (1)
6. **a.** not deep *(key vocabulary)* (1)

Assessment Tip: Total 6 Points

ANSWER KEY

THEME 3

Selection 1

Chinatown

Sample answers provided for questions 1 and 2.

1. In the morning, Chinatown is busy getting deliveries. There are trucks and handcarts in Chnatown. Summing up helps me remember things that happen in the story. *(Reading Strategy: Summarize)* (1 Point)
2. It is a good idea for the boy to stay close to Grandma. This will help keep him safe. *(making judgments)* (1)
3. **d.** parts of Chinese New Year celebration *(categorize and classify)* (1)
4. **c.** He lives in the country. *(story structure)* (1)
5. **a.** activities on a special day *(key vocabulary)* (1)
6. **b.** a place where food and other things are sold *(key vocabulary)* (1)

Assessment Tip: Total 6 Points

Selection 2

A Trip to the Firehouse

Sample answers provided for questions 1 and 2.

1. Why is the pole an important part of the firehouse? Why do firefighters want to be fast? *(Reading Strategy: Question)* (1 Point)
2. The pole is important in the firehouse because it helps firefighters move quickly. *(topic/main idea/details)* (1)
3. **a.** Fire Trucks for Different Jobs *(topic/main idea/details)* (1)
4. **b.** The fire chief greets the children. *(sequence of events)* (1)
5. **c.** special equipment used to do things *(key vocabulary)* (1)
6. **d.** the chief *(key vocabulary)* (1)

Assessment Tip: Total 6 Points

Selection 3

Big Bushy Mustache

Sample answers provided for questions 1 and 2.

1. His dad has a mustache, and Ricky wants to look like his dad. *(Reading Strategy: Predict/Infer)* (1 Point)
2. Answers will vary. *(problem solving)* (1)
3. **a.** He wants to look like his father. *(problem solving)* (1)
4. **b.** at the store *(story structure)* (1)
5. **a.** something people wear to hide what they really look like *(key vocabulary)* (1)
6. **d.** fluffy *(key vocabulary)* (1)

Assessment Tip: Total 6 Points

Selection 4

Jamaica Louise James

Sample answers provided for questions 1 and 2.

1. Answers will vary. *(Reading Strategy: Evaluate)* (1 Point)
2. He must have really liked her idea because he put her name on a golden plaque in the subway station. *(making inferences)* (1)
3. **b.** She works hard on her art. *(making inferences)* (1)
4. **d.** Jamaica draws from the top step of her building. *(sequence of events)* (1)
5. **a.** a piece of metal, like a coin, used to get into a certain place *(key vocabulary)* (1)
6. **c.** a small room *(key vocabulary)* (1)

Assessment Tip: Total 6 Points

ANSWER KEY

THEME 4

Selection 1

Officer Buckle and Gloria

Sample answers provided for questions 1 and 2.

1. I could reread to try to figure things out. *(Reading Strategy: Monitor/Clarify)* (1 Point)
2. The pictures showed the funny things Gloria was doing when Officer Buckle talked. I figured out the children began listening because they thought Gloria was funny. *(drawing conclusions)* (1)
3. **a.** When he checked on her, she would sit at attention. *(drawing conclusions)* (1)
4. **c.** They wanted to see Gloria's tricks. *(cause and effect)* (1)
5. **c.** orders *(key vocabulary)* (1)
6. **a.** a group that listens and watches *(key vocabulary)* (1)

Assessment Tip: Total 6 Points

Selection 2

Ant

Sample answers provided for questions 1 and 2.

1. What are groups of ants called? What are anthills? *(Reading Strategy: Question)* (1 Point)
2. The words, or captions, tell about the picture. The words help me understand more about the story. *(text organization)* (1)
3. **b.** The author tells the important idea and then supports it with details. *(text organization)* (1)
4. **c.** I think ants are a lot like us. *(fact and opinion)* (1)
5. **d.** a kind of plant without leaves or flowers *(key vocabulary)* (1)
6. **a.** long holes under the ground *(key vocabulary)* (1)

Assessment Tip: Total 6 Points

Selection 3

The Great Ball Game

Sample answers provided for questions 1 and 2.

1. Crane is the leader of the Birds. Bear is the leader of the Animals. They decide to have a ball game to settle their argument about who is better, the Birds or the Animals. Summarizing helps me keep up with what is happening in the story. *(Reading Strategy: Summarize)* (1 Point)
2. Birds fly south because they lost the the ball game. This is the penalty for losing the game. *(cause and effect)* (1)
3. **d.** Bat makes his way across the field with the ball. *(cause and effect)* (1)
4. **c.** They both have the idea of a ball game to settle the argument. *(compare and contrast)* (1)
5. **c.** agree to *(key vocabulary)* (1)
6. **b.** an argument *(key vocabulary)* (1)

Assessment Tip: Total 6 Points

ANSWER KEY

THEME 5

Selection 1

Brothers and Sisters

Sample answers provided for questions 1 and 2.

1. Answers will vary. *(Reading Strategy: Evaluate)* (1 Point)
2. Twins have each other to play with. Twins look a lot alike. Twins like to do different things. *(making generalizations)* (1)
3. **c.** Most get along sometimes and have problems sometimes. *(making generalizations)* (1)
4. **a.** Children in Families *(topic/main idea/details)* (1)
5. **d.** only a few days or weeks old *(key vocabulary)* (1)
6. **c.** to get the baby to think about something else *(key vocabulary)* (1)

Assessment Tip: Total 6 Points

Selection 2

Jalapeño Bagels

Sample answers provided for questions 1 and 2.

1. What is a *panadería?* What does the boy need to do before his mother will let him choose what to bring? *(Reading Strategy: Question)* (1 Point)
2. Read all the directions carefully. Be sure I understand each step. Gather all the things I will need. Follow each step in order. Finish each step before going on to the next. *(following directions)* (1)
3. **a.** The bagels would not turn out well. *(following directions)* (1)
4. **c.** They are a mix of two cultures. *(compare and contrast)* (1)
5. **c.** parts of a mixture *(key vocabulary)* (1)
6. **a.** customers *(key vocabulary)* (1)

Assessment Tip: Total 6 Points

Selection 3

Carousel

Sample answers provided for questions 1 and 2.

1. The text says Alex didn't want cake after dinner with just her aunts. She wants someone else to be there. *(Reading Strategy: Predict/Infer)* (1 Point)
2. Answers will vary. *(making judgments)* (1)
3. **b.** She would probably make Alex go to her room for a while. *(predicting outcomes)* (1)
4. **d.** She was upset because her dad wasn't there. *(making inferences)* (1)
5. **a.** a deep moaning sound *(key vocabulary)* (1)
6. **c.** mad *(key vocabulary)* (1)

Assessment Tip: Total 6 Points

Selection 4

Thunder Cake

Sample answers provided for questions 1 and 2.

1. Does everything make sense? If something doesn't make sense, I can go back and reread, or read ahead to see if that helps. *(Reading Strategy: Monitor/Clarify)* (1 Point)
2. She says that if they don't, it won't be a real Thunder Cake. *(sequence of events)* (1)
3. **d.** The girl says she is brave. *(sequence of events)* (1)
4. **c.** Thunder is only a loud noise. *(making judgments)* (1)
5. **b.** a flash or stroke *(key vocabulary)* (1)
6. **c.** the line where earth and sky seem to meet *(key vocabulary)* (1)

Assessment Tip: Total 6 Points

ANSWER KEY

THEME 6

Selection 1

The Art Lesson

Sample answers provided for questions 1 and 2.

1. Answers will vary. *(Reading Strategy: Evaluate)* (1 Point)
2. The author thinks that drawing is fun. He thinks that children should be able to draw whatever they want. *(author's viewpoint)* (1)
3. **b.** to describe something that happened to him as a boy *(author's viewpoint)* (1)
4. **a.** The author writes about his mom, dad, brother, cousins, and grandparents. *(author's viewpoint)* (1)
5. **d.** to hurt or spoil *(key vocabulary)* (1)
6. **a.** a kind of shirt worn over clothes to protect them *(key vocabulary)* (1)

Assessment Tip: Total 6 Points

Selection 2

Moses Goes to a Concert

Sample answers provided for questions 1 and 2.

1. Moses is deaf. He likes to play a drum. He is going on a class field trip to a concert. He knows sign language. *(Reading Strategy: Summarize)* (1 Point)
2. Moses sees that the percussionist has no shoes. She is deaf, too. She feels the music through her feet. *(noting details)* (1)
3. **b.** by holding a balloon; through stocking feet *(noting details)* (1)
4. **c.** They play instruments you hit with something, such as drums. *(making generalizations)* (1)
5. **a.** a quick moving back and forth *(key vocabulary)* (1)
6. **d.** hear *(key vocabulary)* (1)

Assessment Tip: Total 6 Points

Selection 3

The School Mural

Sample answers provided for questions 1 and 2.

1. What are murals? What can you learn from murals? *(Reading Strategy: Question)* (1 Point)
2. Answers will vary. *(problem solving)* (1)
3. **c.** Everyone could help make a mural. *(problem solving)* (1)
4. **a.** They talked about their project ideas. *(sequence of events)* (1)
5. **a.** pictures or views *(key vocabulary)* (1)
6. **c.** the feeling of being proud of something *(key vocabulary)* (1)

Assessment Tip: Total 6 Points

Blending Routine 1

Continuous Blending

Procedure	**Example:** *sat*
1. Display the letter cards or write the letters for the word.	**Display *sat*.** [s] [a] [t]
2. Have children listen as you blend the sounds of the word, "stretching out" the word while pointing to each letter in a sweeping motion. Then say the whole word naturally.	**Point to *sat* and say *sssăăăt*, *sat*.**
3. Repeat step 2, this time having children blend the word with you.	**Children blend *sat* with you, saying *sssăăăt*, *sat*.**
4. Have children blend the sounds on their own and then say the whole word naturally.	**Children blend sat on their own, saying *sssăăăt*, *sat*.**
5. Now have children blend the word silently, in their heads. After they say the whole word aloud, have them use it in a sentence.	**Children look at the letters and then:** • blend the sounds in their heads, saying *sssăăăt*. • say the whole word *sat* aloud. • use *sat* in a sentence.

Blending Routine 2

Sound-by-Sound Blending

Procedure	**Example:** *mask*
1. Display or write the letter or letters that stand for the first sound in the word. Point to the letter as you say the sound.	Display *m* and say /m/. m
2. Have children say the sound as you repeat it.	Children say /m/. m
3. Display the letter or letters for the next sound and say the sound. Then have children say it with you.	Add *a* to display *ma*. Point to *a* and say /ă/. Children say /ă/ with you. m a
4. Model blending the displayed letters, pointing to the letters in a sweeping motion as you say the sounds. Then have children repeat this with you.	Model blending *ma*, saying *mmmăăă*. Repeat. Children blend *ma* with you.
5. Display the letter or letters for the third sound and say the sound. Children say it with you. Have children listen as you blend the sounds so far; then blend together. Add any remaining letters, one by one, and continue this procedure.	Add *s* to display *mas*. Point to *s* and say /s/. Children say /s/ with you. Model blending *ma* and *s*: *mmmăăăsss*. Children repeat. Now add *k* and say /k/. Children repeat. 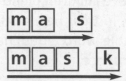
6. Model blending the whole word, pointing to the letters in a sweeping motion as you blend the sounds. Then have children blend the word silently in their heads. Finally, have children say the whole word naturally and use it in a sentence.	Model blending *mask*, saying *mmmăăăsssk*. Children blend *mask* silently in their heads. Children say the whole word *mask* and then use it in a sentence. 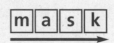

Blending Routine 3

Vowel-First Blending

Procedure	Example: *sat*
1. Display or write the letter that stands for the vowel sound in the word. Point to the letter as you say the sound.	**Display *a* and say /ă/.** a
2. Have children say the sound as you point to the letter and say the sound again. Explain that when you come to this letter as you blend the word, you will remember to say that sound.	**Children say /ă/ as you point to the letter *a* and say /ă/ Say: *When we come to this letter in the word, we will say /ă/.*** a
3. Display the letter for the first sound in the word and say the sound. Then have children say it with you.	**Display *s* and *a*. Point to *s* and say /s/. Have children say /s/ with you.** s a
4. Model blending the word through the vowel, pointing to the letters in a sweeping motion as you say the sounds. Then have children repeat this with you.	**Model blending *sa*, saying *sssăăă*. Repeat, having children blend *sa* with you.** s a →
5. Display the letter for the final sound and say the sound. Then have children say it with you.	**Add *t* to display *sat*. Point to *t* and say /t/. Then have children say /t/ with you.** s a t
6. Model blending the whole word, pointing to the letters in a sweeping motion as you blend the sounds. Have children blend the word with you and then silently in their heads.Have children say the whole word and use it in a sentence.	**Model blending *sat*, saying *sssăăăt*. Repeat, having children blend *sat* with you. Children blend *sat* silently in their heads, then say the whole word. Have a volunteer use *sat* in a sentence.** s a t →

Using the VCCV Pattern

Procedure

1. Write a word with a VCCV pattern. Do not pronounce it.

2. Remind children that each syllable has one vowel sound. Have them identify the vowels. Write a *V* under each one.

3. Have children identify the consonants between the vowels. Write a *C* under those consonants.

4. Point to the VCCV pattern. Tell children that when they see the vowel-consonant-consonant-vowel pattern, they should divide the word into syllables between the two consonants. Draw a slash between the two consonants in the word and between the C's in the VCCV pattern.

5. Cover all but the first syllable. Say it is a closed syllable because the vowel is followed by a consonant. Say that a closed syllable usually has a short vowel sound. Have children sound out the syllable as you point to the letters.

6. Cover the first syllable. Ask whether the second syllable is open or closed. Have children sound out the syllable as you point to the letters.

7. Have children blend the syllables to read the word.

Example: *tablet*

Display *tablet*.

t a b l e t

Mark a *V* below the *a* and *e*.

t a b l e t
v   v

Mark a *C* below the letters *b* and *l*.

t a b l e t
v c c v

Draw slashes to show where the word divides into syllables.

t a b / l e t
v c / c v

Have children blend the first syllable, using a short *a* sound, saying /tăăăb/, *tab*.

Have children blend the last syllable, using a short vowel sound, /lĕĕĕt/, *let*.

Have children blend the syllables in sequence. /tăb • lĕt/, *tablet*.

Teacher's Note

Recognizing the VCCV pattern will help children read many multisyllabic words, even those with elements that children have yet to master. Some exceptions are described below.

- Some words that end in *-ed* are said as one syllable.   Examples: *jumped, ripped*
- Words with two or more consonants (digraphs, for example) may sometimes be divided before or after the consonants.   Examples: *bush • el, ta • ble*
- In words with vowel pairs, the vowel pairs stand for one sound and stay together in the same syllable.   Example: *pain • ful*

Syllable Division Routine 2

Using the VCV Pattern

Procedure

Examples: *final, finish*

1. Write a word with a VCV pattern. Do not pronounce it.

Display *final*.

f i n a l

2. Explain that each syllable has a vowel sound. Have children identify the vowels. Write a V under each one.

Mark a *V* below the letters *i* and *a*.

f i n a l
v   v

3. Point to the consonant between the vowels. Mark a C under it.

Mark a *C* below the *n*.

f i n a l
v c v

4. Point to the VCV pattern. Tell children to try dividing a word with the vowel-consonant-vowel pattern before the consonant. Draw a slash before the consonant.

Draw a slash before the *n* to divide the word into syllables.

f i / n a l
v / c v

5. Cover the second syllable. Say that the first syllable is open because it ends with a vowel. Explain that an open syllable usually has a long vowel sound. Have children sound out the first syllable as you point to the letters.

Have children blend the first syllable, using a long *i* sound, saying /fff ī ī ī/, fi.

6. Cover the first syllable. Point to the letters as children sound out the second syllable.

Have children blend the last syllable, saying /nnnăăl/, nal.

7. Have children blend the syllables to read the word. Ask if it is a real or nonsense word.

Have children blend the syllables: /fī • năl/, *final*. Ask: *Is it a real word you know?*

8. If the word makes no sense, have children divide the word after the consonant. Draw a slash after the consonant.

Display *finish*; repeat steps 1–7. When the word is divided before the *n*, children will conclude that /f ī • nĭsh/ makes no sense. Erase the slash and draw a new one after the *n*.

f i n / i s h
v c / v

9. Cover the second syllable. Say that the first syllable is closed because it ends with a consonant. It should have a short vowel sound. Have children sound out the first syllable.

Have children blend the first syllable, using a short *i* sound, saying /fĭ ĭ ĭn/, fin.

10. Have children blend the syllables to read the word. It should sound like a real word.

Have children blend the syllables: /fĭn • ĭsh/, *finish*. Ask: *Is it a real word you know?*